UNLESS FIRST WE DREAM

The Story of The Great American Flag

By Len Silverfine

Woodbridge Publishers

276 5th Avenue Suite 704 # 944

New York, NY 10001

First Edition

ISBN (Paperback): 978-1-917184-77-9

ISBN (Hardcover): 978-1-917184-78-6

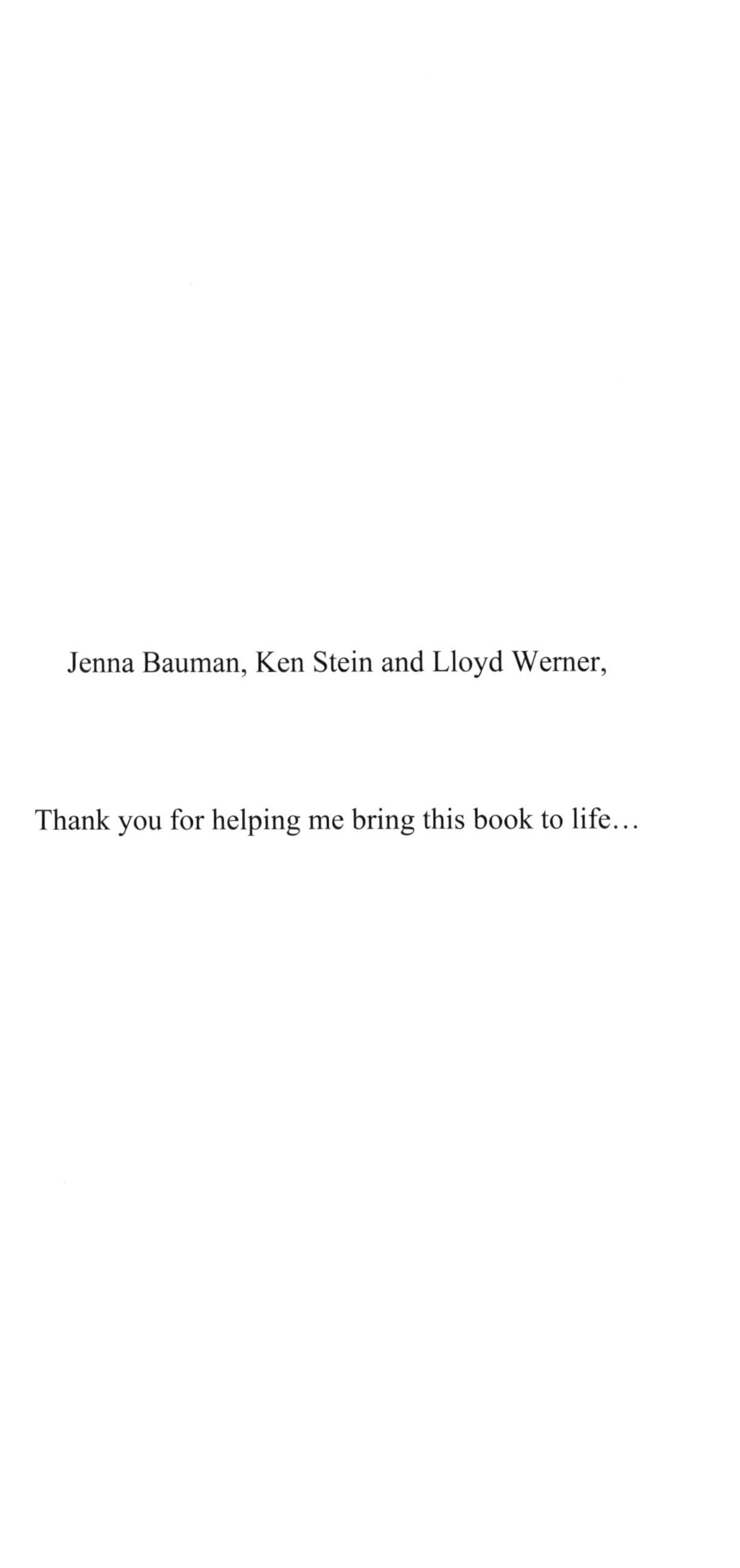

Jenna Bauman, Ken Stein and Lloyd Werner,

Thank you for helping me bring this book to life…

Preface:

You likely have never seen the cover photo until now, a giant American Flag perfectly positioned before America's most famous monument, with the Capital, where we the people are represented, aligned in the distant background. If you are an American, regardless of where your politics may lean, your reaction is probably '*WOW! What a beautiful sight,'* along with a flush of pride.

That's this particular Flag's power, its reason for being, and its story.

—

I'm a marketer by trade, though now 87 and long out of practice. I was a '*Mad Man*' in the Sixties, assigned to some of the biggest package goods, cosmetics, and fragrance accounts in the country. In 1973, as an 'adjunct' professor, I introduced a novel course at McGill University's Business School that received a near-perfect rating of 4.95 out of 5.0 student evaluations. So, while I am comfortable creating a marketing strategy for products and writing advertising headlines and body copy, along with other marketing materials, writing a book is not my forté. Nevertheless, the story of this Great Flag needs to be told, to give credit to those who made it possible, nourished it when it faltered, breathed their hopes and dreams into its mission, and most importantly, in my view, in the hope of reversing America's downward trend.

'*Doomsday prophet?*' Not if you are familiar with history. In the West, there was Rome. And, when it fell, there followed the Dark Ages. Then, in the fifteenth century, spurred on by a prince, 'Henry the Navigator,' Portugal was the first to sail around Africa onto India and the Spice Islands, to attain wealth, and dominance. Isabella of Spain was quick to follow, rivaling and then replacing Portugal's dominance. The Dutch, the French, and the English followed roughly in centurial sequence. And, in due course, in the middle of the last century, we, America, came of age, and world leadership. Need I say/warn that we seem to be falling into the historical pattern?

Can we break the cycle and defy history? Perhaps not. But not to recognize its implications, not to try, and not to pass on to our progeny a sound America, *'a shining city on the hill,'* that's not what we, Americans, have pretended to have strived for since our beginnings.

So, what is my objective in writing this book?

History teaches us that great nations rise and fall. Why they do so can be the result of different factors, but one factor is preventative. The unity of its people, committed to its nation's survival and success is a vaccine against failure. So…

To help Americans see that for our nation to survive and continue to thrive, we must come closer to each other, to the center of our politics, discard extremism, promote compromise, embrace the other, and truly live up to the ideals of our founding documents: The Declaration of Independence, Our Constitution, and The Gettysburg Address.

I can hear your reaction, most politely phrased, '*What a Dreamer!*' Precisely what Carl Sandburg, one of our poet laureates, would say… as he did in his 1922 poem '*Washington Monument at Night*.'

GUINNESS:
THE STORIES
BEHIND THE
RECORDS
1
By Norris McWhirter &
The Editors of The
"Guinness Book of World Records"
Including "How to get into the Guinness Book"

THE GREAT AMERICAN FLAG

The greatest country in the world has to have the greatest flag. This idea does not emanate from the President of the United States, or for that matter from a general in the Army or from an admiral, as one might expect. Rather, it is the guiding inspiration of one loyal American, Len Silverfine, founder of the Great American Flag Fund, who single-handedly organized the building and raising of the world's largest flag.

The story about Len and his flag (or, as he is quick to point out, *our* flag) is the story of one man's dream and determination to restore the nation's sense of unity and the love that Americans once had for their country.

Len, like many Americans, feels that our national pride is rapidly being eroded and that the American consciousness is becoming self-directed. His dream is to unite all Americans by creating a non-political rallying point with a positive image and to rekindle respect for the symbol that once had the power to inspire us all.

The "Stars and Stripes Forever" is not just the name of a famous Sousa march, but what Len's flag looks like when it's on the ground. It covers an area of 86,378.5 square feet, is 210 feet 2 inches high and 411 feet wide. In everyday terms it is a flag that is a football field and a third in length. In a typical suburb, where each house is on a half-acre plot, you could fit four houses with front, back and side yards in the area this flag occupies. It weighs seven tons—one half ton more than the average weight of an African bull elephant (13,000 lbs.) which, according to the "Guinness Book of World Records," is the largest land mammal in the world. The stars, all 50 of them, are each 13 feet in diameter, and if you stack 10½ of our imaginary suburban homes one on top of the other, you will get an idea of how tall the flag is.

The stripes were all constructed from single strips of knit polyester, chosen for its superior strength, flexiblity and ability to stand up to continuous high winds as well as its resistance to the deteriorating effects of air pollution and sunlight.

Stars and stripes *forever* and ever and ever. Two acres of red, white and blue. Len Silverfine's helpers admire the fruit of their labor—all 7 tons of it. These volunteer helpers were able to unroll the mammoth flag faster and straighter than trained teams.

86

Other technical problems, besides the fabric choice, seemed insurmountable. The first flag that Len created in 1976 was raised on the Verrazano-Narrows Bridge (itself a one-time recordholder), which links Brooklyn to Staten Island at the entrance to New York Harbor. It hung for only eight hours before it was blown to shreds while Len and his crew of volunteers watched. It was a highly emotional time for all involved because many months of planning had gone into the project. But more than that, to Len it was symbolic of the deterioration of the fabric of American society.

In no time at all, Len began work on a second flag that was even bigger than the first. He's learned from his mistakes and, instead of using a sailmaker, he enlisted the help of an engineer, Herb Rothman. Herb was the chief engineer and one of the designers of the Verrazano-Narrows Bridge, which Len hoped to make the permanent home of the flag. Herb Rothman volunteered his services, time, and money, and, together with other volunteers, overcame all the problems of construction, storage, transportation, the mechanics of hanging, furling and unfurling the flag, and, of course, locating funds.

During a fund-raising tour, Len's enthusiasm and zeal attracted the attention of the Revlon Cosmetics and Fragrances Corporation's president, Paul Woolard, who gave Len the use of an office at their headquarters in New York, paid his expenses and made the first two major contributions. However, Len worked without salary from 1977 to 1980.

In spite of all the help from Revlon and other corporations, Len found himself in a tight situation on June 14, 1980—Flag Day.

He was to display the flag for the first time in front of the Washington Monument. He had counted on manpower from the various armed forces in helping to unroll the mammoth banner, a job that would take hundreds of strong men several hours to accomplish. But no military men could be obtained!

The flag had to be unrolled before 11 a.m. He had only a few hours to go and the prospects of having the flag set out in time for the ceremonies became dimmer and dimmer.

Flag Day in Washington, D.C. is a big event. People come from all parts

The Great American Flag—bigger and better than ever.

of the country to celebrate and watch the parades. Hundreds of people already had assembled on the green near the Washington Monument—hundreds of people just waiting for the show to start. Why couldn't these people, Len thought, be his helpers instead of being spectators? Here was plenty of people-power, just what he needed, right where he needed it. He grabbed his megaphone and made an announcement to the crowd, explaining the predicament.

Within moments, hundreds of people were shedding their shoes and grabbing a section of the flag. Hundreds of people lined up alongside the rolled-up flag. They pulled, tugged, sweated and yelled. They laughed and moaned and helped each other and finally finished. Trained men, working under ideal conditions and with a knowledge of the situation, do not always roll without a wrinkle the first time, but that's just what Len's corp of volunteers accomplished. They did it right, and they did it in time.

The flag looked so beautiful on the green lawn with the monument behind it that Guinness decided to use the scene as the front cover photo for the 1982 edition of the "Guinness Book of World Records."

Here was Len's dream come true—Americans helping each other and working together. This was not all. Even Len was unprepared for what was the most moving moment of his odyssey with the flag.

Few people in America were undisturbed by the blow to our national pride dealt by the Iranians when they captured our people and held them hostage. When the hostages' release was imminent, Len lost no time in securing permission to display the flag at Andrews Air Force Base. He could think of no more appropriate symbol of welcome for our returning hostages.

In the predawn dark, before the arrival of the ex-hostages, the men of the Ironworker's Union and the American Legion worked up to their ankles in cold mud to ready the flag for the hostages' landing.

When dawn broke, the flag was ready. But tension began to mount when the hostages were delayed.

Hours of waiting ensued. Len and his volunteers finally spotted the aircraft bearing the freed hostages. The plane passed over the flag as it began its descent. Then the plane started to climb again! It gained altitude and passed over the flag a second time.

When the hostages had last seen the American flag it was in flames, burned in front of the American embassy by Iranian students. And now, as their plane prepared to touch down on American soil, they had asked the pilot to delay their long-awaited landing so that all of them could view for a second time that unbelievable moving sight of their flag, the biggest flag the world has ever seen. ■

87

Contents:

Introduction:

America's genius has always been its ability to manufacture unique people out of all manner of raw materials and instill a common, cherished ideal. No nation had done this quite as well. During times of complacency and poor leadership, this genius suffers. Divisiveness thrives. Little feels right. Little seems to go right. We lose our unique character and retreat into tribalism. Suddenly we are not 'the United,' but 'the Red' and 'the Blue,' or even worse, shades of red and blue, and ne'er shall any of the lot agree.

In the latter half of my ninth decade, a member of what I call 'The Luckiest Generation,' that cohort of Americans born just before WWII—and thus, as it would happen—too young to serve in the Korean War, too old for Vietnam, as well as being advantaged by the post-WWII economic boom, where all that was needed was 'the piece of paper' signifying a bachelor's degree to get a promising job. From that point, with grit and smarts (and a good bit of luck, I suppose) to make a decent living, I have a point-of-view about this mess we now find ourselves in.

Let me transport you in time to one of my earliest and, as it turned out, formative recollections. I was playing on the living room carpet in our small apartment on Parkside Avenue, in the Flatbush section of Brooklyn. My mother was vacuuming. Suddenly, she paused and looked at the console radio with alarm. There we were, at war. I doubt that I understood what that meant, but it surely was a 'before' and 'after' timestamp. Over the next few years, as I was learning to read newspapers, the war was foremost to my attention. In those days, New York had The Daily News and Daily Mirror, The Post, The Telegraph-Sun, The Herald Tribune, The New York Times, The Wall Street Journal, and perhaps more that I cannot recall. Our home read The Mirror mostly—a tabloid priced at 3 cents. Their first edition came out the evening before and rushed from the plant in heavy-duty trucks that raced down the avenues, a worker in the rear tossing bound copies to street-corner 'newsstands' and 'candy stores' that quickly stacked, cut the rope ties, and fed copies to groups). After our evening meal and some quiet time, my father would take me with him to the corner store.

MacArthur was evacuated to Australia; Corregidor fell; the 'Death March' began; fear was palpable. Every household received a ration book with coupons for staples, sugar, flour, eggs, and a little meat. It seemed every patch of dirt and windowsill pot sprouted vegetables. Nobody complained. Cars, if you were well-to-do enough to own one, received coupons for gas; the upper half of headlights had to be painted black. Windows required heavy drapes. Air raid drills were frequent, and wardens patrolled the streets, ensuring compliance and shouting out where they saw light. We had all seen photos of the Blitz that devasted London. German submarines were reported to be roaming just off the Long Island coast. There was no screwing around. We were in it together. We were one. 'Americans'. We rallied behind our Flag.

Surely, some were less enthusiastic, but I never saw them. We had 'Block Parties' to buy U.S. war bonds. The barriers between Italian, Irish, and Jewish neighborhoods disappeared. We were in it together. Boys like me accrued bragging rights based on the number of close family members we had in service, and their rank (Marines accrued bonus points). My mother's youngest brother was a major in the U.S. Army. That was big among the boys on my block.

In lieu of endless 'stick ball,' 'punch ball,' 'box ball,' and "stoop ball" games we invented and engaged in with the ubiquitous pink Spalding High-Bouncer, we roamed the streets for discarded cigarette packs, mined the aluminum liners, and formed them into a tight ball. When our pockets could no longer accommodate the ball's size, we deposited the mother lode in the school basement, along with huge piles of newsprint, all of which were collected and recycled for the war effort. We were in it together.

Ebbets Field was just a few blocks up Bedford Avenue. Many of the Dodger stars were off serving in the military. Periodically, the army would stage tactical military exercises in the ball field using blank ammunition to encourage enlistment and promote the sale of war bonds. The stands were full. We were in it together.

FDR was the only president that I knew. I had listened in awe with my family to his fireside chats, as did almost every other American family. He died just shy of my eighth birthday. I wasn't sure about God, but there had always been FDR, who was larger than life to me. So, if I had a religion when I was a young boy, it was America and all it stood for. Over time, I came to think of my bible as The Declaration of Independence, The Bill of Rights, and The Gettysburg Address. (There was a time in grade school when students were required to memorize all three as well as pledge allegiance every morning to the Flag that hung in front of each classroom.)

There was a reckoning for me in the late 60's. I was a 'Mad Man' climbing the ladder at an advertising agency on Madison Avenue. When I would go out to lunch, there were young people like me grouped half in the roadway and half on the crowded sidewalk, somberly reading names of soldiers who were killed in Vietnam, sounding a bell after each name. They were protesting the war. Until that time, it was unthinkable for me to question 'My Country.' It took some time before I joined in the protests, albeit not in the street, but as part of 'Corporate Executives for Peace,' and flew down to Washington to lobby my Congressman and Senators. As I saw it, Vietnam was our 'tipping point'. We were no longer in this together.

The trauma of Vietnam was added to by 'Watergate.' We had a president who had fostered a criminal enterprise and was forced to resign. By this time, I had lost quite a bit of my faith in America, as well as in working my way up the Ad-Man corporate ladder.

Then, whether it was fate or chance, I experienced a sea change—America's bicentennial was approaching. Perhaps this story, conceived during the malaise of post-Watergate, post-Vietnam America, can help us in our current trials to see the importance of compromise and goodwill in a democratic society, the necessity of reducing the pendulum's arc between Left and Right, and the historical reality that great nations rise and fall because the generations that follow the builders soften and lose sight of their foundational dream. As I see it, to be our strongest, we must be united in our vision of being that '*shinning city on the hill.*' I wonder whether there is any American today who would claim we are.

—

Chapter I:

A Big Idea for the Bicentennial

It had all begun innocently enough. A friend, Pierre LeDuc, and I, under the influence of good wine and a carefree day, were in an expansive mood. One of those wonderful give-and-takes where each feed off the other's energy to achieve a level of hilarity and creativity not normally attainable, certainly not alone, nor under usual circumstances.

We were in my renovated barn in Warren; the old Stewart parlor stove glowing, snow falling in big flakes on Main Street, making for a storybook windless Vermont night. It was quite natural for Pierre to comment on how beautiful the village was, and predictable, if you knew Warren, for me to reply: "*You ought to come back to visit on the Fourth... It's the biggest day of the year. People enter floats in the parade. And this year is the Bicentennial!*"

Well, Pierre remarked that he would like to come back, which thrilled me, and that we should enter a float in the parade, which did not. Convinced that life was not a rehearsal, I had set my priorities accordingly. Somehow, a good Fourth had evolved into a celebration of Bacchus rather than the birth of our nation. Entering a float with the intent of winning a grand prize sounded like commitment and work, not my preference for the holiday's activities.

Pierre's first suggestion was for the world's biggest firecracker (as a float that is). I allowed that, as a nation, America had been trying to live that image down for thirty years.

"*How about the biggest Flag?*" he offered next.

"*How are we going to pull that behind my pick-up?*" I parried.

"*Maybe we could roll it down one of the ski slopes?*"

"*Too far from town… Maybe we could pull it behind a plane or helicopter,*" ughh! I was hooked.

The world's biggest Flag stayed in my mind, a germ of an idea gnawing just below the surface of consciousness, popping up every once in a while. A couple of weeks later, alone on the ski lift, between exhilarating runs in near-perfect conditions and legs re-living days of past glory, I was musing about how good life had been to me. How far beyond the experience of my father's life, and how infinitely far beyond that of my paternal grandparents, having crossed an ocean in steerage ('*that section of a passenger ship generally near the rudder, that provides the cheapest accommodations…*'), which toward the end of the twentieth century cannot begin to describe the poverty, the desperation, and the hope it represented at the beginning. I was reminded of how, as a boy growing up in Brooklyn, on Sundays, my father would take me around the city to visit parks, zoos, museums, and monuments. He was a gentle, shy man, not normally given to philosophizing, but on those mornings, we had plenty of time together. He would open up to me in a manner I could not yet fully understand but instinctively valued greatly.

The morning we took the ferry out to Bedloe's (now 'Liberty') Island was the first time he talked at length about his early childhood. He began by telling me of the tiny shtetel in eastern Poland, then part of Imperial Russia, that he had been born into. How my grandfather had avoided the almost certain death of being drafted into the Tsar's army because he was a Jew and because his family would have been imperiled with him away for the years of conscription, by chopping off the ends of the index and middle fingers of his right hand, rendering himself no longer able to fire a rifle. How men came through the village recruiting immigrants to America with tales of '*streets paved with gold*' and promises of unimaginable freedom. How frightened he was as a boy of six when his father left for America! How his mother (my grandmother) and he managed for two years with a newborn sibling on meager rations; the little money my grandfather sent from New York, where he had found employment in a sweatshop, was dearly put aside for their eventual passage to the New World.

Finally, the trek by oxcart at the age of eight, just the three of them, across Poland, Germany, and Holland to Amsterdam; the hunger, horrors, and seasickness of the boat crossing, ending with the incredible joy of seeing the fabled Statue of Liberty as their ship entered New York Harbor when suddenly there was a eureka moment; *the place for the world's biggest Flag was on the Verrazano-Narrows Bridge at the entrance to New York Harbor facing out to sea to welcome the 'Tall Ships' and the World to America's Bicentennial birthday party!*

NB: For America's Centennial, in 1876, the nations of the world that maintained 'Tall Ships' (traditional sailing vessels) took part in a parade in New York's harbor. The grand spectacle was to be repeated.

It was certainly the biggest idea I had ever had, not that I even thought of myself as an idea kind of guy. Pierre was 'the creative', I was the marketing and business part of the team. I wasn't a Flag-waver either. The Sixties and Seventies had disillusioned me like many Americans of my generation, but what it all netted down to was not yet clear to me. The patriotism of my youth had been out of fashion for some time. Cynicism towards America and its traditions was the rage among my peer group at a Vermont resort. The tendency was not to get '*heavy*' about anything other than how to ski the bumps, play the net, or the like. As a somewhat dropout from Madison Avenue, I sensed that if we could pull it off, I might make some money or acquire a measure of fame, perhaps both. My bank account could use the former; my ego, however, mellowed by four years in the Green Mountains, still responded to the promise of the latter, but these were rationalizations subsequently arrived at. The fact was the idea was simply intoxicating! I had no real understanding of what was involved in making such an idea happen. It didn't seem to matter. I was suddenly possessed.

Over the years since, I have often wondered how much the Hollywood 'hero' genre that I subsumed as a young boy was subconsciously responsible for this fateful decision. Gary Cooper could have easily left town with the lovely Grace Kelley and avoided the showdown at '*High Noon*.' But that would not make for a great movie.

—

At the time, I was teaching a course in marketing that I had written for McGill University's Business School in Montreal, where I was working four days a week at Grey Advertising's Canadian office. (McGill's Business School was located just across Sherbrooke Street.) The course, Marketing Planning, was based upon real-life business challenges, not 'book learning,' which was the common practice then. I would divide the class into small groups. Each group would be assigned a marketing problem to solve, either an actual 'live' problem that I would get from my contacts in the business world or an idea for a new product or service that the student group would originate themselves. Each week the groups would discuss their progress in front of the class, following the Objective-Strategy-Execution Plan format: initiating ideas, suggesting solutions, and how they would go about executing all the elements of *their* marketing plan, from determining a *measurable* objective to planning their strategy to achieve the objective, outlining the executional elements needed, and finally establishing the data points that would monitor their success or failure. Their 'final exam' was to present their recommendation and their marketing plan, just as a real-life business group would, to the class. In the case of the 'live' business assignments that we secured, the tasked group would make their presentation to the client at the client's offices, with the class in attendance. Businesses liked participating because they benefitted from the interchange of ideas and, in some cases, recruited students upon graduation. The students preferred the format because it simulated the real-life experience they would shortly face upon graduation. The Dean was ecstatic with the student evaluation and agreed to expand the course to a full-year, two-term course. (I found teaching stimulating and rewarding, so I resigned from Grey Advertising.)

A flood of students enrolled the following term, so we moved from a classroom to a lecture hall and, for my convenience, combined the course into a double session on Wednesday. Additionally, the large class enrollment allowed for two TAs (teaching assistants), both of whom were bi-lingual, as McGill policy at the time allowed students to take exams and write papers in French if they preferred. And, while I had worked at Grey's offices in Paris and Brussels for short stints, much to my dismay, I remained frustrated by my limited linguistic skills beyond ordering a meal and other necessities in French.

At the same time, on Tuesday and Thursday mornings, I began teaching the course at the University of Vermont, located in Burlington. Early Tuesday mornings, I would make the approximate hour-drive from my home in Warren to Burlington for my UVM class. Then, in the afternoon, I would head north for the 90-plus-minute drive to Montreal, where Phil Napier, one of my TAs, offered his couch for my night's stay. On Wednesday, after the McGill lecture and office hours for student visits, I would head south to Burlington, where I was similarly welcomed to use the couch for Wednesday evening in the house of two of my students, West Shell and Brooks Mohrman, along with their housemates. In that case, my ‘fee’ for the evening’s respite was a case of Brador Beer, a cherished Canadian favorite of the boys, unavailable in the States as its alcohol content was 6.2%. Phil, West, Brooks, and their classmates remain dear friends to this day, and without their help, it would have been much harder for me to pursue the idea of a great Flag.

(As an aside, a word about the most unusual ‘live’ assignment ever tackled by my UVM class: Burlington, Vermont, was the location of General Electric’s Armaments Division, which made 20mm and 40mm Gatling Guns for the U.S. Navy. Defense contractors have marketing problems too. Four students decided to see if G.E. Armaments would like to participate. They received a quick ‘yes,’ as every company, regardless of size or business, wants to be involved with their local community.

That final presentation was to be at the G.E. office/factory in Burlington, scheduled for 8:30 in the morning. Of course, everyone, the whole class, had to be present, which meant each student had to have a proper I.D. to pass through gate security beforehand and to be seated in the G.E. conference room by 8:30 a.m. Having been in the National Guard and served six months of active duty in 1961 as a ‘platoon guide’

Chapter II:

'Selling' the Idea

Mondays and Fridays, I was free, and as luck would have it, People's Express, a new budget airline, had just begun to fly from Burlington's airport to LaGuardia in New York City for the very modest fare of $19, which at the time was less than taxi fare from the airport to mid-town Manhattan. And my faithful friend Bill Dowling (Bill and I had started as 'Mad Men' together at Benton & Bowles Advertising in the early '60s) offered me the couch in his apartment on E.71 Street in Manhattan. (NB: adjunct professors make little money and enjoy no job security. Fortunately, however, over the years of my work on The Great Flag, I had friends with couches and spare beds who could afford to pick up restaurant tabs.)

Thus, I began almost weekly trips, sometimes on both Monday and Friday, to Manhattan, first contacting the mayor's office, then the New York City Bicentennial Commission, the Triborough Bridge & Tunnel Authority, and making my way through scores of textile companies, Flag makers, sailmakers, potential corporate sponsors, even the Coast Guard, and a mixed bag of others.

The first big break came with the New York City Bicentennial Commission. I was informed by City Hall that the Bicentennial Commission was responsible for all ancillary events around the 'Tall Ships' celebration. It had taken a few phone calls to get through to the commissioner, Ron Goudreau's office, and then some additional persistence with his secretary. "*We only need three minutes. I promise…We'll introduce ourselves, state our idea in one short sentence… He can say 'No', or 'tell me more,' that's it!*" She finally relented.

I called Pierre, who I should mention is an accomplished artist, and asked him to do two 'storyboards': one of a giant Flag hanging from the Narrows Bridge and another hanging vertically from a cable strung between the twin World Trade Center Towers. As Pierre would be flying down from Montréal and me from Burlington, I arranged to meet him at the Bicentennial Commission's office in lower Manhattan. In the reception area, waiting to be summoned, Pierre unveiled the two concept boards. Not being all that familiar with New York City landmarks, on one of the boards Pierre had placed a giant American Flag hanging from the obscure Bayonne, New Jersey Bridge. Normally, I would have been amused. Just then, we were summoned.

We entered the Commissioner's office, introduced ourselves to Goudreau, and I said, "*We want to hang the largest American Flag, a Guinness world record, on the Verrazano Narrows Bridge to welcome the Tall Ships and the World to America's biggest birthday party!*" (I think I held the storyboard of the Bayonne Bridge in hand without revealing it.)

Goudreau's eyes widened, and he quickly asked, "*Can you do it?*"

Without hesitation, I replied, "*Yes!*" (Of course, at this point, we had no idea what it would take or if it was even possible. Details. Hadn't we put men on the moon just a few years prior?)

"OK, I'll put you in touch with the head of the Triborough Bridge and Tunnel Authority," responded Goudreau.

Bingo! That was it. All of three minutes. (Hey, Goudreau had a lot on his plate.) We managed to retreat from his office before jumping up and down and high-fiving it.

A couple of days later, while I was in class at UVM, the Dean's secretary walked in, clearly annoyed, as we were not supposed to receive calls during our classes. And, frankly, I didn't even know the Dean's phone number. *"There is a man on the phone for you who says he is in charge of a bridge and cannot wait until you end your class,"* she said.

I excused myself from the class, which was already buzzing, and walked down the hall to the Dean's office.

"My name is George Schoepfer. I run New York's Triborough Bridge & Tunnel Authority. We're in charge of the Verrazano Bridge," said the voice over the phone.

I replied, *"We want to hang the world's largest Flag on the bridge to greet the Tall Ships. Can the bridge handle that?"*

"My bridge can handle anything! When can you come down?" he asked.

Schoepfer's briskness should not come as a surprise from a man who ran an enterprise that collected tolls on seven bridges and two tunnels in New York City and was the protégé of Robert Moses, the first TB&TA chief, considered one of the most powerful people in New York City and the State's histories. (Personally, I had a beef with Robert Moses, as he was behind the move of my beloved Brooklyn Dodgers from Ebbets Field, 6 blocks from my childhood home to Los Angeles.)

I called Pierre, who naturally booked a room in the swank Pierre Hotel on Fifth Avenue, and we arranged to go down to New York to meet George Schoepfer the next Monday. Actually, I liked the idea that Pierre was staying at The Pierre, one of New York's finest hotels, a very respectable address to give for our pickup, as Schoepfer had mentioned that he would send a limo for us.

Monday morning arrived. Pierre and I walked out of the Pierre lobby, and there was the limo. When we finally made it to the V-N Bridge, it was around 9:30 a.m., and there was still some rush-hour traffic. The administrative building is on the Staten Island side, so we had to first drive across the bridge. We approached the other side, where the toll booths are located, and our driver opened his window and motioned to a policeman, who promptly walked out on the roadway and stopped all the Brooklyn-bound traffic so that we could cut across the lanes and get to the admin building. We were certainly feeling like '*bigshots*'.

We entered a large room with quite a few staff sitting at desks monitoring television screens on the wall in the front of the room (this was early 1976; the computer age was in its infancy). I introduced Pierre and myself to Schoepfer. After shaking hands, he turned and shouted to the room, '*Close the Upper Roadway!*' OK, the rush hour had just about ended, but still… This was the biggest bridge in the world!

We drove out across the now-empty upper roadway, got out of the limo, and George gave us a primer on the bridge and its construction features. Let me say that walking on the now empty upper roadway of the world's biggest suspension bridge one feels tiny, and a bit in awe of the engineering required to produce such a magnificent structure.

—

Chapter III:

The Planning

We began discussing where and how to rig a giant Flag. It quickly became apparent that our original idea to make a Guinness World Record Flag, which was then held by the J.L. Hudson Department Store in Detroit, at approximately 24,000 square feet, displayed every Fourth hanging down the side of the store, would look tiny on the V-N Bridge. *Three times that area would be more like what was needed.*

J.L. Hudson Department Store Flag, a Guinness record holder at 24,000 sq. ft. The Verrazano-Narrows Bridge needed to be 3 times that or 71,000 sq. ft. to make an impression.

A couple of weeks later, we returned for an engineering meeting. Herb Rothman, the bridge engineer who took over from Othmar Ammann after the world-renowned suspension bridge builder died, ran the meeting. Herb quickly pointed out that a steel cable rigged from the tops of the towers spanning the distance of 4,260 feet (60 feet longer than the Golden Gate Bridge) would be enormously heavy and expensive to rig and would sag of its own weight to lay down on the roadway. Herb had even invited two Dupont engineers in hopes that their new miracle fiber, Kevlar, might offer a solution. Again, the distance between the towers proved far too great. The best option seemed to be to hang the Flag from the lower level of the bridge. If positioned near the Brooklyn Tower and allowing for some clearance above the water, there would be more than half a mile of leeway remaining for the Tall Ships to enter the harbor. Some weight would have to be added to the Flag's bottom to minimize the wind effect, but the Flag would hang freely and could be retrieved easily enough if needed. That became the plan.

I consulted the Yellow Pages (again, this was 1976) and searched for flag-makers. The Annin Flag Co. in New Jersey seemed to be the biggest. I called and inquired if they could make a flag roughly 70,000 sq. ft. At first, they thought this was a crank call. When I convinced them that I was serious, they pointed out that they were in the lead-up to the Bicentennial and were overrun with orders for American flags. Further, they suggested, given the size of what we had in mind, that I might do better talking to a sailmaker. I did some more research and ended up contacting Hood Sail in Marblehead, Massachusetts. It was early spring, and Hood was experiencing unusual demand for new sails and spinnakers because many sailboat owners planned on being on their boats in New York Harbor for The Tall Ships and wanted new, in some cases artistic, attention-getting sails, so they too were jammed with orders and declined. However, Hood directed me to a small group of freelance sailmakers, former employees, that they thought might be able to take on the project. The freelancers said OK and were able to secure enough red, white, and blue 3-ounce spinnaker fabric to do the job. The cost, I believe, was $3,000 for labor; the fabric was donated.

At this point, I was making routine trips down to New York on Mondays and/or Fridays. On one of the trips, George Schoepfer gave me an extensive tour of the Verrazano-Narrows bridge, including taking the small elevator in one of the bridge's towers up to the top and a visit to the Staten Island anchorage, where the bridge's four 36-inch-diameter steel cables, each bundling close to 28,000 pencil-thick steel wires, are 'anchored,' as they are also on the Brooklyn side. The anchorages are secured by a grand total of some 730,000 cubic yards of concrete. (Along with, it is rumored, some unsavory mob victims that 'dropped in' before the mix hardened.)

Note that the Golden Gate Bridge, being a single-level span, has two 36"-diameter cables, and its span is 60' shorter than the Verrazano-Narrows.

Incidentally, typical of suspension bridges, the Verrazano-Narrows bridge span between towers rises and falls above the mean high-water level between the warmest and coldest days of the year as steel expands and contracts. In the case of the Narrows Bridge, its height above the mean high-water level of the harbor can change by as much as 13 feet. That is why, when you drive over this and other suspension bridges, you see interlocking tooth sections of the roadway just under the towers, to allow for this expansion and contraction.

I also remember being told that the Bridge Authority had self-insured the bridge against any catastrophe, as the only real threats were **a very large ship running into the concrete and rock bumpers surrounding each tower or *a fully fueled large jetliner hitting one of the bridge's towers.***

All seemed to have come together for a '*go-ahead*' six weeks prior to the Fourth. We were then informed that we had to get final approval from the Coast Guard, as they were the authority in charge of the Tall Ships parade and, of course, the harbor. The Flag hanging from the lower roadway would narrow the passage under the bridge for the Tall Ships. As stated earlier, we thought we had provided adequate allowance, over a half mile, in our plan by choosing to suspend The Flag close to the Brooklyn tower, leaving more than enough room for the Tall Ships to maneuver even in adverse weather. However, the Coast Guard Commandant was adamant that the sailing ships might, in severe conditions, need all the leeway between the towers. (I could not help but wonder if such severe conditions were forecast whether the event would be postponed, but to be fair, were I the Coast Guard Commandant with all this responsibility that day, I would be overly cautious as well.)

That left us, just weeks away, with only the option—a poor one at that—of raising The Flag up between the suspender ropes of the Southside main cables, a fixed rather than free-waving position. In retrospect, it was a gamble with poor odds, but at the time, no one wanted to kill the idea of a giant 'stars and stripes' greeting the Tall Ships, and I don't recall anyone raising the issue. The flag was already near completion in Marblehead, Mass., made with 3-ounce nylon fabric, commonly used for spinnaker sails. Delivery was promised for June 27th, and a trial run for the next day, the 28th.

—

Chapter IV:

The Test Run

Warren, VT, has a small airport for a few private, single-engine planes and some gliders. I got in touch with one of the plane owners, who had a Cessna that accommodated four. Two friends, Charlie Brown and Sparky Potter, were photographer enthusiasts who took photos in the Mad River Valley all through the year and put together slide shows that were aired locally for entertainment. Of course, they didn't want to miss this opportunity—a photographer's dream. Each, with two Nikon cameras dangling from their necks and a bag loaded with rolls of Kodachrome film and extra camera lenses, flew down with me in the hired Cessna. In those days, there was a small airport in Flushing, Queens. We were met there by Bob Martin, the TBT&A Chief of Maintenance. From Flushing, we made our way south and west to Brooklyn and the Verrazano-Narrows Bridge, where the outside New York-bound Lane of the upper roadway had been closed to traffic and The Flag lay accordion-folded on a long flat-bed truck.

June 26 started out as a gorgeous, warm, sunny, windless day. It was quite a sight to see workers attaching The Flag to winches every 50 feet along its full length and see it slowly lifted from the truck's bed.

Euphoria swept over the work crew and late morning drivers on the bridge, who slowed, honked their horns, and cheered wildly as The Flag was slowly hoisted, 13-foot stripe after 13-foot stripe, by eight winches that climbed up the clusters of bridge suspender ropes spaced every 50 feet. A magnificent, powerful, and inspiring sight, with the sun's rays gleaming through the nylon spinnaker fabric.

Photo by Charlie Brown/Sparky Potter, Waitsfield, VT

Photo by Charlie Brown/Sparky Potter, Waitsfield, VT

Photo by Charlie Brown/Sparky Potter, Waitsfield, VT

Photo by Charlie Brown/Sparky Potter, Waitsfield, VT

Photo by Charlie Brown/Sparky Potter, Waitsfield, VT

Photo by Charlie Brown/Sparky Potter, Waitsfield, VT

Within two hours, however, euphoria changed to concern and then nightmare as it became apparent The Flag could not be retrieved. A modest wind that would have posed no threat to The Flag's originally intended manufacture and placement, hanging freely from the bridge's lower roadway, was fatal to its fixed placement within the suspender ropes. The Great Flag tore apart over the course of that warm summer afternoon in pieces so huge that we had to rip them further into manageable size to bring the tattered remains safely onto the bridge deck. I don't recall ever feeling worse than I did that day. Given the agony of America's schism during the 70's, the symbolism of a giant American Flag blowing apart was particularly troubling, and I didn't need anybody to point a finger at the chief perpetrator. I left the bridge devastated and full of shame, wishing only to hide in the darkest, most forgotten corner.

(An aside, I later requested one of the destroyed Flag's stars, which I brought back with me on a trip down to New York in my pick-up. We displayed it, standing up and supported by a large wood frame, in the 1977 Warren July 4th parade and donated it to the Warren elementary school to be hung on their gymnasium wall. I don't know if it still exists.)

That evening, at Bill Dowling's apartment, I received a call from Bob Martin. Saddened by the day's events, he wanted me to know that the TB&TA switchboard was deluged with callers, as were all the New York TV and radio stations. A wide variety of individuals, groups, and businesses were volunteering to help, offering to sew the flag together in time for the Fourth. There were offers from ladies' auxiliary groups, scouting troops, religious organizations, and even one from the owner of a sportswear factory in Brooklyn with the necessary facilities and forty seamstresses, all of whom had volunteered to work round-the-clock to repair The Flag in time for the Tall Ships Parade on the Fourth. Of course, this was not possible and not even advisable for fear of a repeat casualty that would mar the day's celebration. We needed to go back to the drawing board and re-engineer the concept. I thanked him, hung up, and turned to Bill. "*It's like I have touched an exposed nerve. I've started something much bigger than I ever imagined. I can't leave it like this. I must finish it.*"

What had begun as an idea for a spectacular greeting to the Tall Ships and the World to America's 200th anniversary had, in its poignant failure, touched an exposed nerve of love of country in post-Vietnam, post-Watergate America. For myself, having been raised in the era of American ascendancy by parents who were very thankful for their good fortune and recognized that with a good thing comes responsibility, I just couldn't walk away. Then too, the germ of a grand vision was taking hold.

Carl Sandburg may well have captured the essence of this eclectic, wonderful country of ours when, standing before the Washington Monument, he said, "*The Republic is a dream. Nothing happens first unless first we dream.*"

How true I felt. Thirteen colonies, emerging victoriously from their revolution, were significantly different in size, terrain, population, religious beliefs, economic interests, and climate, not to mention how they treated race and human rights. They banded together not out of common practice or mutual love *but out of fear of the British, French, and Spanish acquisitive imperial behavior of the time, which they had good reason to fear would gobble them up one by one unless they came together as one.*

(Remember, at the end of the 18th century, Canada to our north was part of the British Empire, which had only a few years earlier wrested it from the French. Florida to our south part of the Spanish. And everything west of the Mississippi belonged to the French Empire.)

Can you imagine writing a constitution for that disparate group of colonies? They didn't want another king, but should it be a Republic or a Democracy? In a pure democracy, laws are made directly by voters, i.e., every voter has a vote of equal force. The majority decides; the minority is pretty much unprotected. In a republic, voters elect representatives who represent them and make laws according to a constitution that protects minority rights from the will of the majority.

As a kid, I thought America was a pure democracy—that every adult citizen had a vote of equal force. And that if you were an American, you would enjoy the same freedoms and rights wherever you lived. Only later did I learn that in reality our arrangement was not quite that simple.

The United States has a hybrid government, partially republican and partially democratic—what some term a 'Representative Democracy,' and with some unique quirks. For example, we have an Electoral College system for the election of our presidents (and vice presidents). The Electoral College consists of 538 electors, (same as the total for House and Senate members), the number of which does not change as the total population may grow or decrease (unless, I suppose, if more states were added?), nor does it change as some states may gain and others may lose population. Each state is allotted two votes for their senators, plus votes for each of their members sent to the House of Representatives. The number of House members is determined by the decennary (10-year) census. Though, no matter how small the population a state has one House Representative and therefore three Electoral College votes.

For example, currently, Wyoming has one Electoral College vote for its population of approximately 582,000 people plus two for its senators, while California has 52 and Texas has 38 electoral votes, two for their senators plus one for each of its approximately 765,000 inhabitants. (Hey, marriage requires some compromises. And, in the case of the victorious colonies, there were 13 betrotheds.)

Thus, our election system can be confusing. And as was the case in 2016, a presidential candidate could win the popular vote in a national election but lose the Electoral College vote and the election according to our Constitution's rules.

Given these anomalies, all of us, every American, have but one common, unifying symbol. We all 'march' to and salute the same banner, The Stars & Stripes.

When taking this into consideration, Sandburg's notion is not far-fetched. 'America' is a dream, and like all dreams, if not nurtured and reinforced, they can turn into nightmares.

—

Chapter V:

The Rebirth

The Verrazano-Narrows Flag, the vision of uniting post-Vietnam and post-Watergate America, had succumbed to poor design, modest summer winds, and an over-eagerness to celebrate a very significant national anniversary. But, in its spectacle of failure, it had awakened a somewhat dormant communal spirit, the vital ingredient, the glue needed to hold the United States together as one nation, one people.

So, the vision, or 'dream,' if you will, was that a new *Great Flag* could become the catalyst for rallying Americans together. If *We,* as in *We the People*, could set about to build an even bigger flag, one that would redeem and enlarge upon the first attempt, the size and boldness of the gesture could become the symbol by which *We the People* picked the fallen flag off the battlegrounds of the Sixties and Seventies and restored it to its proper place, mending the wounds of Vietnam and Watergate. Naïve, hopelessly romantic, of course, but quintessentially American—even more far-fetched, I knew in that instant, '*felt*' in my gut, that if that vision could be kept pure and unsullied, somehow, in some way, the force of the idea would capture enough imaginations to prevail. Forty-eight years later, despite all the ups and downs, I still feel that way, but my feelings have gained urgency as our divisiveness has grown.

The days following the Bicentennial were the beginning of hard lessons in reality. Commitment to designing and building a new Flag that would be able to be unfurled on most flag holidays was hard to come by. George Schoepfer, Executive Officer, and Chief Engineer of the TB&TA, in tears with the rest of us on the bridge, did not hesitate to promise that he would continue to provide whatever support he could. And he was to do so over the next few years, even after it became necessary to change the destination of The Flag from the Narrows Bridge.

Herb Rothman, of Weidlinger Associates Engineers, agreed to head up the technical committee we were forming of experts from various textile companies to design a new Flag that would meet the needs of the unique task.

If the project was to get anywhere, it was clear that a major benefactor was required. We had one very effective tool with which to work. Charlie and Sparky, my photographer friends from Warren, Vermont, had clicked through some 40 rolls of film, capturing The Flag as it was slowly being raised, when it was fully unfurled, and in the agony of blowing apart. They put together a powerful Audio-Visual (A-V) slide show enhanced with stirring music by Sparky's wife, Peggy Potter. (Again, this was 1976, long before home computers, iPhones, and computerized software revolutionized and facilitated such presentations.) I saw the effect of The Flag Slide Show firsthand when they decided to air it publicly at the local Warren nightspot, *The Blue Tooth*. It seemed the whole Mad River Valley turned out—not just the regular Saturday night revelers, but native Vermonters that were never seen at '*The Tooth*.' The audience's response was spontaneous and overwhelming. From pot-smoking hippies to grizzled farmers, in that moment, we were all one, fiercely proud Americans!

I began to write, call, visit, and follow up with scores of corporations, media sources, patriotic groups, philanthropists, and politicians, for the most part with no success. Eventually, my advertising background paid off.

My last assignment at Grey Advertising, New York was running the Revlon Cosmetics account. That was in the late 60's. Almost ten years later, my contacts were now highly placed. I arranged a presentation of The Flag Show at their offices in the General Motors building. They were impressed and wanted to help. Sanford Buchsbaum, Senior Vice President, remarked to his colleagues, "*Guys, sometimes it is more than about lipsticks.*"

By chance, Revlon had just made a major commitment to support the 1980 U.S. Olympic effort, the first by a cosmetics company. If I could find a way to tie in The Flag, they had a budget for that. I was uncomfortable with 'commercializing The Flag,' i.e., having a particular company or group sponsor it. To my mind, the vision for the great Flag required 'purity' to have force. And 'purity' meant that it welcomed and belonged to all Americans without preference (the classic example being the Statue of Liberty; she belongs to us all).

However, I did come up with an idea (with help from Pierre) for Revlon to sponsor a world's record television commercial, '*A Salute to the U.S. Olympic Team.*' The 30-second spot would open with an establishing shot from a helicopter of a large crowd, then zooming in to reveal a few thousand school kids performing a record-breaking 'card-stunt,' first forming a giant 'U.S.A.,' followed by the Olympic five-ring symbol, and finally an American Flag, all over the soundtrack of '*America the Beautiful.*' I was becoming hooked on 'big ideas,' patriotic and participatory ones at that.

Revlon didn't exactly say yes, nor did they say no, so I started researching the production, and they slowly, almost reticently, got into it. (NB: At no time did I 'sell' this TV commercial idea as if I were an advertising agency. I never asked for a fee.) They gave me the use of an office and picked up my out-of-pocket expenses associated with the TV commercial idea.

Eventually, 6,000 students at the University of Southern California volunteered to perform the 'card stunt' during halftime of a U.S.C. vs. Cal football game at the Los Angeles Coliseum (despite the Dean's absolving himself of responsibility: "*We've never done a card stunt anywhere near that large. And, usually, half the kids have had more beer than they can handle...The other half are tossing the cards around like Frisbees. Tell 'em they'll be on television, and a whole row of frat boys will stand up, turn around, and moon the cameras.*")

Well, they did it—set a free-world record for a card stunt, that is, not moon the TV cameras. The Dean was proud as a newborn father. The '*Today Show*' ran an 8-minute piece. NBC's 'Nightly News' ran 4 minutes. 'PEOPLE' magazine did a page entitled, *'Len Silverfine thinks not just big, but colossal—from flags to football stadium card stunts*.' (Now, I was really hooked!). The Goodyear Blimp donated footage to establish the zoom-in. The Mormon Tabernacle Choir OK'd their recording of '*America the Beautiful*' for the soundtrack. And Screen Extras Guild forgave the $90 per head extras fee, which would have amounted to over $500,000.

There were actually three card stunts in the commercial, followed by a salute from Revlon…

The Olympic Salute

The salute to the U.S. Olympic Team was another big idea.

ITS OBJECTIVE: To dramatize Revlon's support of the U.S. Olympic Team, and single out their sponsorship of the 1980 Olympic Games.

It was the free world's largest card stunt, performed by 6,000 student volunteers of the University of Southern California.

It also had the most participants of any television commercial ever produced.

It required the cooperation of the U.S. Olympic Committee, Screen Extras Guild, The Mormon Tabernacle Choir, ABC Wide World of Sports and the Goodyear blimp.

It received a full 6 minutes of network coverage on the "Today Show", plus 4 minutes on "Nightly News".

And, Revlon was given credit for sponsoring "The Olympic Salute" event and television commercial.

HAPPY

His flag on the Verrazano-Narrows Bridge (above) was a triumph for Len Silverfine (right) until wind destroyed it. Bouncing back, Silverfine assays his handiwork (below) in the L.A. Memorial Coliseum. Revlon's film of the stunts will be used to promote the Olympics.

LEN SILVERFINE THINKS NOT JUST BIG BUT COLOSSAL—FROM FLAGS TO FOOTBALL GAME CARD STUNTS

Remember the impossible dreamer who hung a 366-by-193-foot American flag from New York's Verrazano-Narrows Bridge back on June 28, 1976—and watched the wind rip it into tatters within hours? Well, Len Silverfine, 41, is at it again. Two weekends ago he staged the biggest stadium card stunts ever attempted east of Peking. One purpose was to promote his efforts to hang another giant flag, and the scene was a University of Southern California football game. "It won't work," warned Dr. James Dennis, director of campus life and recreation at USC. "Someone is bound to drop his pants for national TV." But 5,600 students hoisted their cards without incident—shaming the previous free world record of 3,700.

Silverfine, a onetime account executive and college lecturer, said he was delighted. Soon he hopes to persuade Revlon, which filmed part of the extravaganza for an Olympics commercial, to help underwrite another Great American Flag Project. The huge Stars and Stripes, like its ill-fated predecessor, would be displayed next July 4 at the entrance to New York Harbor as a tribute to Silverfine's father and millions of other immigrants. It will be reinforced with steel and nylon ropes and will be 20 percent larger than the Bicentennial failure. The new flag will cost $300,000, and though Silverfine hasn't yet lined up backers, he's not worried. "I haven't felt this good," he announced after his triumph in Los Angeles, "since the morning of June 28, 1976." □

"People" magazine November 13, 1978

Revlon, credited as the sponsor, was gracious in their thanks. The following week, its Chairman, Michel Bergerac, handed me a check made out to the newly formed non-profit Great American Flag Fund in the amount of $50,000. They also gave me an office and consulting agreement with clear instructions to work on The Flag project when I wasn't helping Revlon with Olympic promotion ideas. And the Revlon finance department took over responsibility for the Flag Fund's accounting. My high school pal Ken Stein and his law firm Greenfield, Stein & Senor registered The Great American Flag Fund as a 501(c)(3) non-profit and took on the fund's legal responsibilities.

Lloyd Werner, another high school pal of mine, now a broadcast television executive, and Bill Dowling, a rising executive in the hospitality business, along with George Austin, a business executive, joined Ken and Herb Rothman on the Flag Fund's board. Having three of my closest friends, serious businessmen, on the board gave me comfort that my failings would be kept in line.

Paul Woolard, Revlon's President, agreed to be Honorary Chairman of The Great American Flag Fund, and Bergerac along with other Revlon executives began to open additional corporate doors, which brought in Ed Pratt, CEO of Pfizer, who also became a forceful champion of The Great American Flag.

—

Chapter VI:

The Engineering & Manufacture

Meanwhile, Herb Rothman developed a plan to safely "fly" the Flag from the suspender ropes (this time with adequate engineering of The Flag's fabric, construction, and rigging—unfurling, furling, and storage). Herb's plan was designed to fly The Flag in winds as high as 25 mph and be able to retrieve The Flag safely even in winds as high as 30 mph, which, if forecast, would nix any unfurling plan (most flag holidays are in months that average lower maximum wind velocities). When not in use, The Flag would be automatically drawn down neatly into a 400' long waterproof steel container securely stored at its base, resting upon the bridge's south-side longitudinal girder.

This was basically the same positioning as the first flag; however, we wanted to not only give the new Flag proper manufacture and rigging but also increase its size to '*…be bigger and better*,' so The Flag's width was extended 50' to the next group of suspender ropes, which meant when conforming as close to U.S. Flag dimension proportion standards as possible, The Flag's area would increase from approximately 71,000 to 86,000 sq. ft. (roughly two acres or nearly two football fields in area).

As you might expect, the fabric, construction, and specifications were severe and beyond the purview of a bridge engineer. Enter Fred Fortress, a highly regarded textile industry expert affiliated with the Philadelphia College of Textile and Sciences. Fred, a wonderful man, opened an especially valuable door, without which I am not sure the new Flag would have been possible. He managed to secure 15 minutes on Roger Milliken's calendar for me to make the pitch. Milliken was the textile industry's single most respected and influential individual. If we could bring him on board, the other textile companies essential to the project were sure to follow.

I flew down to Spartanburg, S.C., on an early morning flight from La Guardia, loaded with 70 lbs. of aluminum cases and a backpack holding slide projectors, a tape recorder, a dissolve unit, and the Brown/Potter slide show that had proved to be so effective in bringing in people. We had trimmed the Flag Show down to 9 minutes, which only left

5 for the pitch. Not much, but I knew by now that if a viewer wasn't hooked in the first few minutes, it didn't matter. It would never be their thing.

At exactly 12:15 p.m., 'Big Red,' as he was known, walked into the auditorium, followed by an orderly mob of employees. (I learned later that he had simply gathered them up as he passed desks like a Pied Piper in Milliken Company's 'open office' environment.) Fifteen minutes became thirty as Mr. Milliken asked questions, with not a stir among the audience. Afterward, I was invited to join the Milliken Executive Committee for lunch. Following lunch, those employees who had not seen the first performance were crammed into the auditorium for a second showing.

In May 2007, after I finished an initial draft of 'UNLESS FIRST WE DREAM,' I sent a copy to Mr. Milliken. He replied a couple of days later.

MILLIKEN®
Roger Milliken
Chairman

May 29, 2007

Mr. Len Silverfine
202 South Street, #1
Sausalito, CA 94965

Dear Len:

Thanks very much for sending me the tremendous story on your participation and leadership of the Great American Flag endeavor.

When I got it (and in spite of the fact I did not have any time), I read it all the way through and found it absolutely exciting and inspiring.

Thanks for being the trash mover that you are and what you did to incite a feeling of patriotism, much needed, into the daily lives of so many.

I hope you find another similar project that you can work on and use your talents for the betterment of the USA.

All the best,

Roger

Roger Milliken

Milliken & Company, 234 South Fairview Avenue, P.O. Box 3167, Spartanburg, SC 29304 (864) 503-2811
Fax: (864) 503-2970

Milliken & Co. made the Great American Flag the theme of its annual industry show, typically an adaptation of a Broadway musical designed to introduce the new line of Milliken products, which is performed each year in a New

York theater for the buyers, etc., of Milliken fabrics. Even the theater's curtain was transformed into an American Flag.

As Fred had predicted, the textile industry quickly rallied. A group of twenty or so experts from a dozen different companies began meeting monthly at Revlon's Board Room on the 46th floor of the General Motors Building in New York. Every aspect of the new Flag's construction and display, from the choice of fabric (13 oz. polyester used in the manufacture of commercial "grass-catcher bags") to the selection of the dyes to the thickness of thread and the type of stitching to be used, was thoroughly discussed and evaluated for the task. In addition, seat-belt webbing was used along the borders, and heavy vinyl collars were used where holes were needed to accommodate the steel rigging for raising and lowering The Flag.

In almost every sense, The Flag's specifications represented unique challenges. The sheer size dwarfed any textile product ever sewn. Each stripe, now 16' wide, would require four strips of 50-inch-wide fabric (allowing for overlap for three rows of chain stitching in each seam). The Flag's position on the bridge and exposure to the elements meant that the dyes used had to hold their colors as true as possible.

The stripes were 412 feet long (the bridge's suspender ropes, clusters of four steel 'ropes' suspended from each of the two main cables, the outer clusters attached to the lower roadway, and the inner clusters to the upper roadway were grouped approximately 50' apart. We allowed a bit extra for billowing). That's a lot of very long seams to sew. Mistakes were out of the question since the arms of the sewing machines accommodated a limited amount of fabric between needle and post. N.B. Anchor Industry's plant had commercial heavy-duty sewing machines. However, given the limitations of their factory's floor space, they decided that instead of pulling fabric through the machine as it sewed, they would build a cart for the machine to move through the fabric. As sewing progressed from one edge and yards and yards of fabric accumulated, there was no practical way of correcting an error made earlier.

Anchor Industries employees with their creation.

I remember joshing the shop foreman of Anchor Industries in Evansville, IN, where The Flag was sewn, when we first viewed it in its entirety, laid out that "*…one star is upside down!*" He turned to me without even looking at The Flag and replied in measured tones, "*I've checked and rechecked the stars over a hundred times…They're right!*" It seemed that I wasn't the only person beset by nightmares of making an embarrassing and unforgivable mistake.

The foreman then told me of the peculiar labor problems he was encountering in his plant of 250 workers. Because only one sewing machine could be used (due to the limited distance between needle and post as well as the need for the machine to move through the fabric), the crew was necessarily limited to a handful. Yet, every Anchor employee wanted to play a part. At the change of work shifts, employees would line up outside his office to beg for work on The Flag, some with tears, offering to work for free. If you were to open the vinyl collars sewn into The Flag, you would see the names of workers and their families surreptitiously etched in with enormous pride.

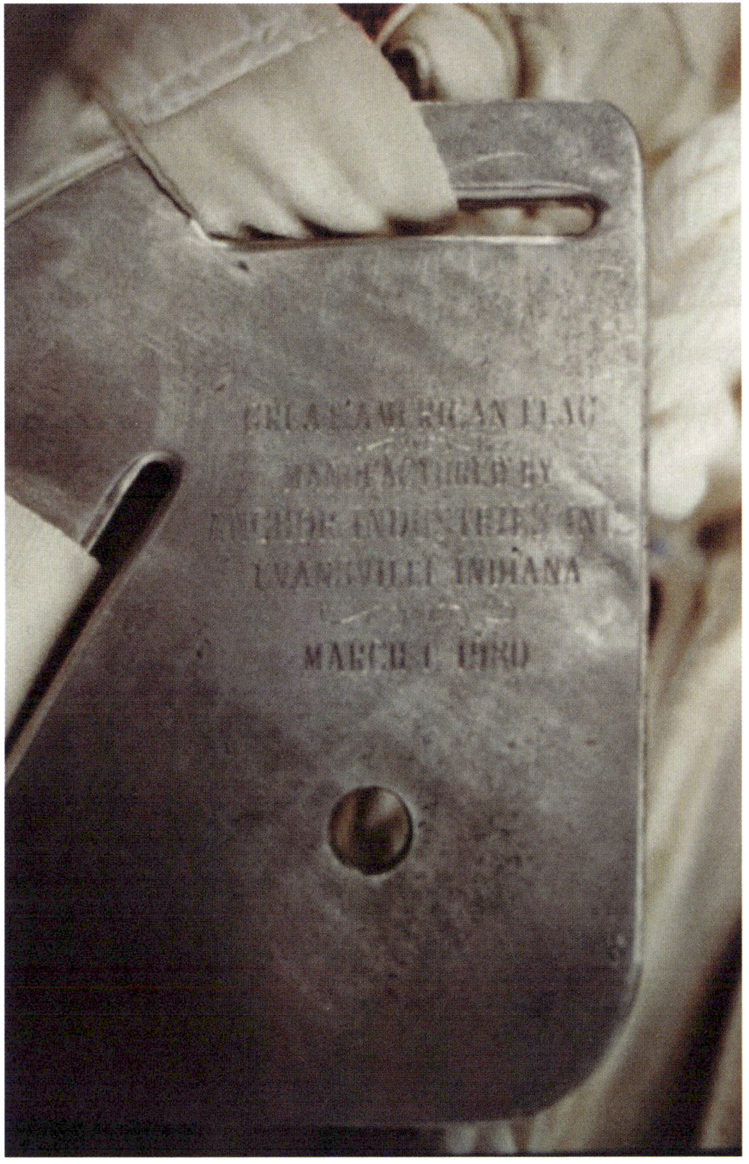

Manufacturer's label held in place with seat belt webbing.

There was one incident, in the course of the project that makes for quite a story. When I was in New York and staying with Bill Dowling, one of Bill's friends owned the "hottest" restaurant on the upper East Side. The place was always packed, but the owner would sit Bill and I at a large round table in the front reserved for his friends. We would never be billed for drinks, just food, and we would meet some very interesting people.

One evening I was seated next to a guy who asked me about the Flag project, specifically about the fabric being used. I told him it was 13 oz. grass-catcher fabric. He said you mean Raschel knit polyester. I replied yes as I had remembered that term being used in one of the Tech committee meetings.

He then asked me if I had a sample of the fabric, which I did happen to have. "Why don't you bring the sample to my house…I want to show you something that could be a problem."

He gave me his address on Sutton Place. For those that know Manhattan, Sutton Place, a small street adjacent to the East River in the 50's is *The* Manhattan address. The east side of street is all town homes that have backyards overlooking the East River.

I called Herb Rothman figuring that I would need someone with lot more tech knowledge than I had to attend the meeting with me. A few days later Herb and I went to Sutton Place. The lots on the east side of the street are narrow so the town homes butt up against each other, albeit each one appears more handsome than the other. Norman (last name Alexander) greeted us and took us for a tour of his home first. It was exquisite in every regard – stone quarried in France, oak for floors, walls, stairs, and bannisters from French forests, etc. Everything custom and hand-crafted. After the tour he said let's go up to the library. The elevator was a bit small for three of us, so he sent Herb and I up to the library and graciously walked up the stairs himself.

We sat down and Norm enlightened us that he had designed a factory in Germany to manufacture Raschel knit fabric. Construction took a couple of years, in which he was required to live in Europe in the event he was needed. He had taken the time to design and source materials for this home and had all the stone, wood from ancient oak trees, etc. shipped to New York for this house.

He asked if I had bought the fabric sample, which I did and handed to him. He put reading glasses on, studied the fabric, picked at a thread and pulled the piece completely apart, just like the old comedians used to do to with a loose thread on a man's suit jacket, except in this case Herb and I were not laughing.

Needless to say, as soon as I got to a phone, I called one of the textile experts on the committee. He investigated it, and yes, Norman Alexander turned out to be a famous textile engineer, and yes it was possible to unravel a piece of the fabric as he did, but given the construction of the flag, there would not be any openings, like the fabric sample we used, to pick at a loose thread. PHEW! Australia wouldn't be far enough for me to hide.

—

Chapter VII:

The Fundraising

The textiles and materials finally selected were largely stock items or based upon existing technology, and the companies involved contributed them generously. Therefore, in terms of cash, we only needed about $50,000 for the actual manufacture of the Flag (to refer to it as 'sewing' would not do justice; we were way, way beyond Betsy Ross). Celanese had located a suitable manufacturer, Anchor Industries, in Evansville, IN, and picked up that cost. However, the rigging, which needed to be robust and manufactured to unique specifications, rose to over $500,000 (reminder, these are 1979 dollars). On top of this were operating expenses beyond what was being picked up and donated 'in-kind' by Revlon, Pfizer, and others involved. In short, we were in the fund-raising business.

To be sure, the notion persisted that the project would inspire the public to send in their dollars like the Statue of Liberty Pedestal Fund of a century earlier. However, such dreams, I quickly learned, require substantial promotion, public relations, and media coverage. For America's Centennial France had commission the sculptor Frédéric Auguste Bartholdi to design and build Liberty as their gift. However, America had to decide where to place Liberty. It was decided that Bedloe's Island in New York Harbor, adjacent to Ellis Island, where the greatest number of immigrants passed through, was most suitable. Further, a pedestal had to be built upon which Liberty would rest. Liberty's Pedestal Fund of the 1880s was successful because Joseph Pulitzer and his NEW YORK WORLD newspaper drove the funding as part of a circulation promotion that lasted months. Donors' names, regardless of amount, appeared on the front page of THE WORLD.

With no Pulitzer in sight, we decided to broaden the base of corporate donors to underwrite a public appeal for the funds needed for the rigging. To this end, we thought up major public relations events to showcase The Flag and attract individual donations, but also to give credit to corporate sponsors, who, if they donated $25,000, would become 'Star Sponsors.'

The perfect view of The Flag on the bridge would be from a ship at the harbor's entrance. I imagined The Flag's debut (then optimistically targeted for July 4, 1980) serving as the backdrop for a television special from the deck of an aircraft carrier anchored before the bridge (not unlike the opening scene in the movie 'Patton'). Of course, entitled '*Stars and Stripes Forever*,' and hosted by Bob Hope, as those old enough to remember World War II and the Korean and Vietnam Wars would recall, Hope was famous for hosting these patriotic extravaganzas.

Accordingly, one of the first steps was to secure an aircraft carrier. With help from an ex-D.O.D. (Department of Defense) executive working at Revlon, I began writing to the Navy. Specifically, to Admiral David Cooney, who was then the Navy's Director of Public Information. I received a reply that the Admiral agreed to see me in the Pentagon. I took AMTRAK down, lugging the slide show cases and backpack. (The memory of carrying that load through the interminable corridors of the Pentagon remains.) After I had set up the Flag Show, the Admiral had marched briskly into the conference room, followed by a phalanx of crisply dressed aides in descending rank order. I sensed his immediate coolness to my informal appearance. I was still going down to New York each week from Vermont. My beard, somewhat trimmed from its ripest days, was still full, my hair long, and my dress was a step up from work jeans, which was not exactly what the Admiral was accustomed to. I kept my opening remarks brief and trusted the emotion of The Flag slide show to work its magic.

Adm. Cooney warmed visibly when the lights came back on. Blunt and to the point, he asked, "*Young man, what do you want from me?*" Just as direct, I replied, "*An aircraft carrier.*" Blood seemed to boil up his neck all the way to his forehead. His considerable frame appeared to grow larger as he levitated out of the chair. At the same time, his aides seemed to cower down in fear. For what seemed to be several minutes, he delivered a tirade, bemoaning the public's lack of understanding of how under-fulfilled the Navy's fleet requirements were and how audacious my request was, then changing his tone with "*…and now, young man, I'm getting out of here before I lose an aircraft carrier!*" And with a smile and a warm wink, he was gone, followed by his minions. Two weeks later, a formal letter arrived from the Commander of the North Atlantic Fleet stating that an aircraft carrier had been reserved for Fourth of July duty in New York Harbor.

I had less success getting through to Bob Hope, but I did get a call from Elizabeth Taylor's assistant. Liz had heard of the plan and wanted to co-host the show with Hope, whom she would contact. This was her way of celebrating her newly won American citizenship. (She was born in Great Britain.) The event of course never materialized, but Admiral Cooney and Elizabeth Taylor both would play crucial roles later, providing vital assistance to The Great Flag's odyssey.

—

Evansville, having a relatively small airport, had just a couple of hotel options nearby. As it happened, reporters, photographers, and TV crews covering the event were all staying at the same hotel as myself and two Flag Fund staffers. We were all eating at the small hotel restaurant the evening before, sharing stories. An ABC TV producer approached, and unlike others, he seemed to have a negative impression of the project, and everyone involved with it. He had been briefed in New York by Hughs Rudd (a powerful ABC-TV news commentator) that he wanted some footage to back up '*trashing'* the project in his regular Sunday evening broadcast that weekend. I was totally bewildered as to why anyone would want to do that, and I gave the ABC producer a lengthy account of the project. He realized that what he had been told was way off base and vowed to put together a positive video clip, despite Rudd.

The following Sunday night, to his millions of viewers, Hughs Rudd derided "*this 7-ton plastic Flag... will do about as much good as a bumper sticker that says, 'Honk if you love Jesus.'*" I beg to differ with Mr. Rudd. The video footage behind the commentary showed a glorious Flag being proudly unfurled by a snappy crew of Anchor employees to the applause of a considerable crowd of

Evansville, Indiana, onlookers. In my innocence, I thought Rudd's criticism an isolated incident.

After the Evansville event, The Flag was packed into a donated 40-foot-long trailer with side panels beautifully adorned by a local muralist and moved to a truck park in Evansville to await further instructions.

—

Chapter IX:

Lesson in Reality

As someone new to the non-profit fundraising business, it hadn't occurred to me that there was a finite sum of money available from corporations for which non-profits competed, which meant that it was not unlike the for-profit marketplace. A new entity into the market represented yet another competitive threat for the scarce dollars that corporations set aside for charitable donations, much the same as a new toothpaste brand represented a threat to those brands already on the market. And, in the case of a giant American Flag, there were some who did not see its value in inspiring and bringing Americans together for a common cause. What they did see was a competitor, and an unworthy one at that—*a 7-ton plastic Flag that could/would divert charitable funds from their project.*

I did discover who was behind the effort to stop The Great Flag project. Ironically, he was a partner in an advertising agency that I had work for early in my MadMan career, although my contacts were with the other two partners. He was now leading the cleanup effort of a part of Manhattan that much needed cleaning up. That did not, in my view, excuse his *trashing* of the Flag project. When I confronted him, he replied: "*Didn't I see that the American flag was the symbol of every imperialistic venture we have ever taken.*"

I don't know how to talk to people like that. I feel blessed to have been born an American. I accept that my luck comes with obligations. I am obliged to defend and improve America. So, where one man sees a *7-ton plastic Flag*, *as a symbol of imperialism,* I see a gorgeous, giant inspiration reinforcing my ideals and inspiring me to fulfill my obligations to the nation of my birth *albeit that nation is imperfect as we all are*.

And yes, that is a dream, but one that walks in the footsteps of good company. Did not our Founding Fathers have a dream when they wrote our Constitution? And Lincoln with his Gettysburg Address. Martin Luther King had a dream as well.

To my mind, if more Americans could be inspired to accept and nurture our national dream, all manner of needs, from curing diseases to renovating decaying cities to protecting our nation, would be more easily accomplished, and we would fulfill our ideal of being *that shining city on the hill.* Of all the media attention The Great Flag received, perhaps this article by Julian Morrison portrayed the story most accurately.

★★★ Reaching for the

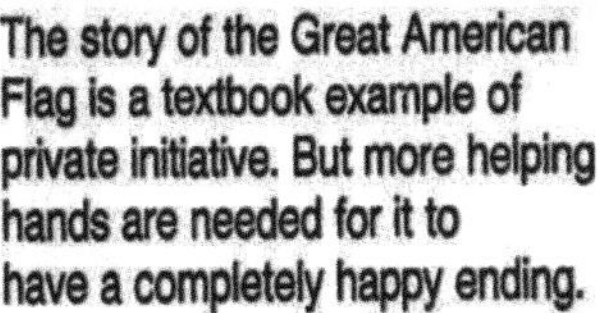

The story of the Great American Flag is a textbook example of private initiative. But more helping hands are needed for it to have a completely happy ending.

The world's biggest flag was first unfurled in an Evansville, Ind., parking area. Anchor Industries workers wore special footgear to protect the cloth.

By Julian Morrison

IT'S A PRODUCT of private initiative and inventiveness, of unblushing patriotism. And of perseverance after heartbreak. It's the Great American Flag—the biggest flag in the entire world.

Into it have gone the efforts of some of the top minds in commerce and industry, advertising and academe. Old soldiers and young children have given money to it. Seamstresses, ironworkers, dye makers, weavers, secretaries and truck drivers have worked on it.

JULIAN MORRISON *is a free-lance writer based in Washington, D.C.*

It started out as a small idea in a small New England town five years ago. Len Silverfine, an ex-New York City advertising man who was lecturing on marketing at Montreal's McGill University and living in Warren, Vt., began wondering what he might contribute to the town's bicentennial parade. He was thinking in terms of something he could pull behind his pickup truck. Nothing spectacular, just something pleasing and patriotic and maybe a bit unusual.

The flag turned out to be more than a bit unusual. A lot more. It quickly passed pickup-class size, outgrew Warren and swept beyond New England.

Stars With Old Glory ☆☆☆

Silverfine assembled a small group of volunteers and made a 71,000-square-foot flag of nylon taffeta. And since Silverfine's idea by then was to make the flag America's 200th birthday greeting to the world, the only place to unfurl it was the great bridge that vaults the Narrows, the entrance to New York Harbor.

Putting the flag on the 2-mile-long Verrazano-Narrows Bridge—the flag was stretched over cables—ended in disaster. The 3,000 pounds of red, white and blue fabric ripped to shreds with an avalanche of sound on a flawless June morning just six days before the Tall Ships sailed into New York. A mere 7-knot breeze had done in the Great American Flag.

Or had it? Before sunset Silverfine was back thinking, dreaming, planning. Object: A new version of the flag that would not be a tragically temporary feature of the bridge, a flag that would be around for a long, long time. Silverfine went looking for help.

He found Paul P. Woolard, president of Revlon Cosmetics & Fragrances, U.S.A., a man who categorically rejects the word *can't.* After conversations with Silverfine, Woolard began working with him on a campaign to raise funds and attract volunteers to produce the new flag and put it on the bridge. The flag would be unfurled on all national holidays and on special occasions.

Then Woolard recruited Edmund T. Pratt, Jr., board chairman of Pfizer. Pratt listened to Woolard's reasons for involving themselves and their energies in an affair that had absolutely nothing to do with either company. He signed on immediately.

Says Woolard, "Ed Pratt and I have a lot in common. We think the timing is very right to stand up and salute the flag in some unusual but appropriate fashion and to be proud of the flag, corny as that may sound."

Pratt, whose company has been part of New York for more than 130 years, felt he and Pfizer owed the city a certain debt. "We wanted to help restore some of the luster to the Big Apple, and I just thought this was an exciting thing," he says.

"I'm committed to focusing on the pluses about our country. We've had a defeatist complex in the country and the city here, more than Americans like to have, and I think a few things, such as this flag, that remind us of the greatness of this land are worth doing."

The talent hunt next found Fred Fortess, director of textile and apparel research at the Philadelphia College of Textiles and Science. Fortess joined the spontaneous chorus of "you've got to be kidding" that invariably greeted Silverfine's pitch. Then he went to work.

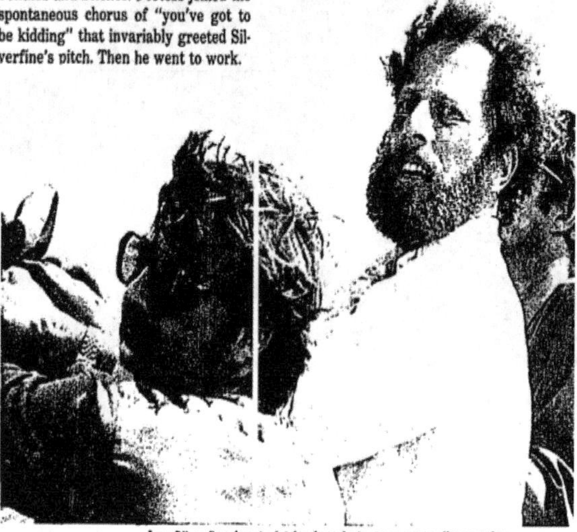
PHOTO: GREAT AMERICAN FLAG FUND

Len Silverfine (center) tries in vain to save an earlier version of his creation. A breeze ripped the flag to shreds when it was displayed on the Verrazano-Narrows Bridge in June, 1976.

Fortess soon had a committee of textile experts going full blast: Edward Kubu of Allied Corporation; Norman Vandervoort of Belding Corticelli Thread Company; J. Donald Keen, Robert Stultz and Gilbert Bell of Celanese Fibers Marketing Company; Peter Kennedy and Gary L. English of Du Pont; Robert Leonard of Milliken & Company; and John Skoufis of Sandoz Colors & Chemicals.

Key to the committee's work was Herbert Rothman, senior partner of Weidlinger Associates and one of the engineers who designed the Verrazano-Narrows Bridge. His role was to ensure that the committee's flag would be compatible with their creation. You don't attempt to casually attach what amounts to the world's biggest sail to just anybody's bridge. The rigging had to be exactly right, ready to raise and lower the flag when needed. In addition, permanent housing to store the flag had to be built on the bridge.

The fabric chosen by the committee is something you may have around your house. It's the stuff lawn mower grass-catcher bags are made of: Lots of air gets through, but the grass stays inside.

Rothman insisted on strength of a minimum of 100 pounds per linear inch for the fabric and the seams, and the committee came up with a knit polyester weighing 13½ ounces per square yard. It allows passage of more than 200 cubic feet of air per minute through every square foot of the huge flag—"a very necessary property," says Fortess, "if the flag is exposed to winds up to 40 miles per hour" that could sweep through the Narrows. The knit of the cloth also allows it to stretch 50 percent in one direction "to permit some ballooning so the flag will have the appearance of billowing."

Then came the matter of dyes and a dyeing system to produce reds and blues that matched the official flag color standards. And the committee had to select the proper thread, seam design, reinforcing tapes and rigging connections. The tapes turned out to be automobile seat belt material.

There remained the ultimate question: Who was going to sew this gargantuan banner?

Don Keen of Celanese suggested Anchor Industries of Evansville, Ind., as much, he said, "for the spirit of their people" as for their ability to carry out unusual tasks.

"Like the sling we made for a guy who wanted to raise his sunken yacht," explains Anchor Vice President Eric Soelter, who welcomed the challenge (although he admits to initial disbelief, the same as everybody else). The flag thrilled Anchor's employes as much as it did Soelter and the company's president, John Daus, Jr.

SUDDENLY they were drowning in more than 11,000 linear yards of 50-inch-wide fabric knit by Milliken from 12,000 pounds of Allied Corporation's polyester filament yarn. And out of that ocean of cloth they were being asked to stitch a flag 210 feet by 411 feet—larger even than the original because Silverfine wanted this flag to symbolize the American tradition of doing things bigger and better. It would be more than 86,000 square feet, the size of two football fields. With the webbing and the rigging grommets in place, it would weigh approximately 7 tons. And the Anchor people loved it.

Soelter says, "You really became emotionally involved when you saw the reaction it got—everyone was asking, 'When is it my turn to sew?' 'When can I work on it?' It was just tremendous. Everybody wanted to be involved."

They had their hands full. "The seams were 411 feet long, so we rigged up a stand and put the sewing machine on wheels, and rather than pull the fabric through the machine, we pulled the machine through the fabric."

Another problem: "When you do something like this, you have to plan every step and then check and double-check yourself because it's so big, you can't actually see whether you have the stars in the right places or the right number of stripes," Soelter says. "It's like a puzzle.

"We inspected every inch of every seam, but the floor area of the factory was only 5 percent of the flag's area, so we got 60 or 70 people in a long line and pleated the flag back and forth across the floor until we'd inspected all of it."

At one point Soelter had 300 T-shirts printed with the slogan, "Anchor Team—Great American Flag," and passed them out to the employes. On one recent day he spotted three employes wearing theirs in the plant, even though the flag had been completed in March of last year.

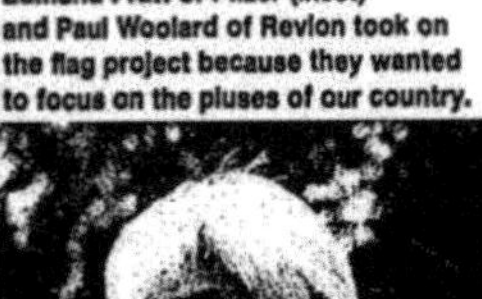

Edmund Pratt of Pfizer (inset) and Paul Woolard of Revlon took on the flag project because they wanted to focus on the pluses of our country.

PHOTOS: GREAT AMERICAN FLAG FUND

THIS IS THE HEART of America, he says, "and these are the kinds of people who built this country. An opportunity to make a contribution like this comes along only once in a lifetime, and I think these people realized it. The excitement it generated, not only in the plant but also in the community, was something to see."

That same excitement had earlier infused the committee, Soelter remembers. "Here were people with a high degree of technical knowledge from different companies that compete with each other in the open marketplace. But when it came to a project like this, they worked as a team."

The original target date for raising the new flag on the bridge was July 4, 1980. That goal wasn't met because the complex rigging to raise and lower the banner had not been built. "I thought we'd be swamped with contributions from the people," Silverfine says, "but the press portrayed it as just a big flag not as the symbol of this country's greatness it's meant to be. And the money just didn't come in."

The flag, folded up inside a Fruehauf trailer, has been hauled by a Preston Trucking Company tractor to a score of cities and sometimes been unfurled—on the ground—in the attempt to get contributions. Last month backers again displayed their masterpiece in Central Park in hopes of collecting funds to construct the rigging. The project was also plugged on national TV.

But hundreds of thousands of dollars are still needed.

Woolard insists, "Nobody—nobody—is in this thing for commercial reasons. Revlon got involved because somebody had to, and it's up to the corporations in this country that think the way we do to become involved and provide the rest of the money for the project. But we'd love it if thousands of individuals gave a dollar apiece." [Contributions may be sent to the Great American Flag Fund Inc., 767 Fifth Avenue, 49th Floor, New York, N.Y. 10022.]

He sums up, "The cause is right. It's just the time to say we're proud of our country, whatever difficulties we may be going through. It's time to say we're proud of America." □

To order reprints of this article, see page 58.

Chapter X:

The Roadshow

The Great Flag effort was now tainted with controversy. A New York Times article, as well as the ABC-TV Hughs Rudd piece and a later article in the Wall Street Journal, killed our fund-raising efforts. Our "friend" was well-connected politically. The Flag remained in its trailer in Evansville, with no funds available to move it east across the country.

Back to the well again, I called bedrock supporters to see if we could raise the money to truck the Flag east. I thought that if it were moving, visiting towns and cities along the way, it would attract the media and the support of everyday Americans. Bob Stultz of Celanese was the first to call back: "*Len, I've gone on the line to my CEO. I've bought you two weeks of trucking. Best I could do. You'll have to leverage that.*"

Once again, when there seemed to be no hope, a champion appeared. This was the scenario that constantly repeated itself throughout the years. The Great American Flag was more difficult to define than to feel. It was a completely American phenomenon; many Americans would not, *could not*, let it die. By now, I was fully aware that this was the real worth of the project. Beginning with myself, thousands of ordinary, and some not so ordinary, Americans found in this intangible idea not a giant Flag per se but a way to express their feelings, *the dream they held,* toward the country they loved. That was the magic of this Flag, and, in truth, every American Flag. And precisely what Carl Sandberg had in mind!

We went first to Indianapolis, followed by Lexington, Cincinnati, Charlotte, Spartanburg, Philadelphia, and Providence. In each city, we opened the rear of the trailer, pulled out the corner of the Flag, and displayed a star. Firemen and laborers were always there to help. Schoolkids and passers-by were always attracted. Local papers always published an article, and television stations would grant interviews on their talk shows.

Left page of spread in Philadelphia College of Textiles and Science journal showing students revealing one star.

AMERICAN FLAG

The flag covers over two football fields of ground and weighs 14,000 pounds. It is scheduled to be hung on the Verranzano Narrows Bridge in New York on July 4, 1980. The flag is being carried across country in a semi-truck called the "Flagship". On its Journey to the bridge it will visit several cities. On May 19, 1980, the flag will arrive at the Philadelphia College of Textiles and Science, and it will also be featured in the Memorial Day Parade at the Independence Mall in Phila.

Right-hand page of spread in Philadelphia College of Textiles and Science journal showing The Flag, Fred Fortress, and its trailer being inspected by students and families.

It was late May, and no longer could I delude myself into believing that money would pour in from a sympathetic public. Enthusiasm was ebbing, even among fervent supporters. I sensed the project would not survive missing another Flag Day or Fourth of July without being displayed to national attention, generating credibility and momentum.

—

Chapter XI:

On to Washington

I flew to Washington. In a few short weeks, with the help of Willard Marriott's 'Honor America Society,' The American Legion, Building & Construction unions, corporate supporters with D.C. connections, and most importantly, Admiral Cooney, who managed to upgrade the Defense Department's normal, low-key celebration of Flag Day from a modest parade of troops on The Ellipse to a major event with all the military service bands, including The Old Guard Fife and Drum Corps in their Revolutionary War dress, at the Washington Monument.

The Ironworkers agreed to provide a crew, and the American Legion promised to deliver volunteers to help with the unfurling. This was the spring of the Iranian hostage crisis and the trauma of a failed rescue attempt. Bureaucracy and officialdom were trumped by Americans just wanting to do something positive and uplifting for their country.

Shortly after 5:30 a.m. on June 14th, I arrived at the Monument grounds. The sun had just risen over the Capitol Building as I crossed the L'Enfant East-West axis that bisects the Mall, stretching from the center of the Capitol dome, through the Monument, on through the Reflecting Pool, to the precise middle of the Lincoln Memorial. Like many Americans, I regard our 16th president as one of our greatest leaders. Reflexively, I glanced west, and to my delight, the sun's rays, at dawn's low angle, aligned perfectly, piercing the portal of the Memorial. The Great Emancipator, for an instant, was brilliantly illuminated (shades of Stonehenge and the Pyramids). It was a good omen.

We managed to unload the Flag from its trailer thanks to a dozen hefty Ironworkers and a construction crane donated by a Virginia operator who had heard our radio appeal the day before. However, we lacked enough manpower for the unfolding. We thought it would require a minimum of 50–60 able men, spaced evenly over the length of the Flag, to distribute the stress of pulling on the fabric (I think Anchor Industries had employed a similar number of employees at the Evansville airport unfurling). It was almost 9:00 a.m. The military parade, I was curtly reminded in no uncertain terms by the '*spit and polish*' Major, Tom Groppel, in charge of the ceremony, *"...We will commence promptly at 1040 hours, with or without your Flag!"*

The Legion's bus arrived with a small number of veterans. As appreciative as I was for their effort, I wasn't sure which war they had fought in. They needed chairs, not a work assignment.

A bit frantic by now, I looked around for help. The only place with a crowd at that time of the morning was at the base of the Monument, where early tourists formed a long line waiting to take the elevator to the top. I picked up a bullhorn and pleaded: "*Folks, we're a little shorthanded this morning. We could sure use some help rolling out this big Flag. If you'd like to give us a hand, please come on down, take off your shoes, and pile them up by the man with the raised arm, and line up along the edge of the flag."*

Scores of parents, grandparents, and their children came running down the hill, removed their shoes, and worked patiently for 40 minutes until we had the Flag perfectly aligned with the Army surveyors' pegs, perpendicular to L'Enfant's imaginary line on the West Slope of the Monument Grounds. There was even a group effort to help a blind volunteer play his part in the unfurling. Watching that enthusiastic cross-section of America come to the rescue and handle 7 tons of red, white, and blue was an inspiration for all. When we were through, I walked back to the speaker's platform just in time for the start. Major Groppel was there, shaking his head and saying, "*I've seen it all now... Anytime you need help with that Flag, count me in!*"

I was ecstatic. Here was *proof of concept!*

Tourists that had been in line to go up the Monument came to the rescue.

The Old Guard Fife and Drum Corps.

—INTERNATIONAL—

Herald Tribune

Published with The New York Times and The Washington Post

PARIS, MONDAY, JUNE 16, 1980

BROAD STRIPES — The world's largest American flag is unfurled on the Mall near the Washington Monument for Flag Day. Former advertising executive Len Silverfine hopes the 210-by-411-foot polyester banner will wave from New York's Verrazano-Narrows Bridge soon; he hung a smaller flag there for the U.S. Bicentennial, but the wind tore it to shreds.

Soviet Bid to Crush Party Feud Seen

Afghan Regime Executes 3 Amin Aides

By Tyler Marshall

NEW DELHI, June 15 (LAT) — The Soviet-backed Marxist regime in Afghanistan has tried and executed three former Cabinet ministers, Kabul radio announced yesterday. All three men were loyal to President Hafizullah Amin, who

control, Parchamite leaders, including Mr. Karmal, were outmaneuvered in the struggle for power. Leading Parchamites were first banished to East European ambassadorships and later purged. Those returning home or remaining in Afghanistan were subject to imprison-

all elements of the party. But there was little willingness to forget past differences, political analysts believe.

In recent months, a number of reported incidents indicate that members of the Khalq faction were involved in attempts to undermine the Karmal regime.

PLO Called

Israel Co[...]

EEC Mid[...]

By William Claiborne

JERUSALEM, June 15 (WP) — The Israeli Cabinet condemned the European Economic Community's declaration on the Middle East today, likening it to the 1938 surrender of the Sudetenland at Munich.

The Cabinet ministers also agreed that if the EEC attempts to send a fact-finding mission to the Middle East it will not be accepted in Israel, Cabinet sources said.

[The Palestine Liberation Organization, meanwhile, joined other hard-line Palestinian guerrilla groups and Syria today in rejecting the EEC's views on the Arab-Israeli conflict, United Press International reported from Damascus. The PLO, saying the EEC approach to the situation in the Middle East was in line with the Camp David peace plan, called on the Western European nations to free themselves from U.S. influence.]

Prime Minister Menachem Begin, in language that seemed unusually strong even for Israel's outspoken Cabinet, said the declaration adopted Friday by EEC leaders in Venice "calls upon us and all other nations involved in the peace process to involve the Arab SS, called the Palestine Liberation Organization."

Mr. Begin noted that el-Fatah, the main arm of the PLO, declared at its recent annual meeting in

EEC

U.S.

BONN, Ju[...]

Ironworker Union magazine cover.

The perspective of this photo certainly portrays The Flag's great size.

—

Sure enough, Gulf & Weston's P.R. man called not ten minutes later, major irritation in his voice. "*You caused some commotion here this morning. Mr. Bludhorn came tearing out of his office into mine, wanting to know why I hadn't said yes to begin with. You had better come over in the morning so we can begin planning this luncheon!*"

"*I'll make it up to you. John Young and Robert Crippen just agreed to be guests of honor... Only let's make it a brunch... We must get them out to JFK to catch the 2:00 p.m. Concorde flight to Paris.*"

I released the news to a New York Post reporter I knew. The next morning, the Mayor's and Parks Department staff had a sudden attack of interest in helping to plan the event. (I just love the way some of our world works.)

The heavens opened early on June 2nd. By 5:00 a.m., it was coming down in torrents. Willard Scott, NBC's weatherman, and the Today Show crew were there, as were more than enough Building & Construction Trades union volunteers. We all found shelter and waited, but the downpour never let up. It didn't dampen enthusiasm, though. All agreed to come back when the event was rescheduled. The brunch went ahead with light attendance. Only those top executives with limos, plus a lot of Gulf and Western employees rounded up at the last minute to fill tables, attended. The next day, city bureaucrats got over their cooperative spirit and were stone-cold to rescheduling.

—

Chapter XIV:

Liz Saves the Day

Elizabeth Taylor was appearing on Broadway in "Little Foxes" and would have been an honored guest at the June 2nd event if not for recuperating from a bout of pneumonia. I called her assistant and asked her to mention the predicament we were in. Liz called back and said she would be delighted to attend when the event was rescheduled. Plus, she offered some ironclad *"Rain Insurance"*. "*Send me a couple of Great Flag 'T' shirts. Size XL, I'll try to get Dolly to attend as well. If it rains, you won't have to worry about anybody leaving*." The lady was not only beautiful; she had a delightful sense of humor. My adoration from pre-teen years on had been justified.

I couldn't help telling of her offer to appear with Dolly in Flag 'T' shirts and soon got a call from the head of the New York/New Jersey Trade Unions begging me to kill the story out of the fear he *"wouldn't have a man on the job anywhere within 50 miles of Manhattan."*

Dolly Parton couldn't make it, but Liz showed up—and yes, in a Great American Flag 'T' shirt. The sun shone all day long.

Elizabeth Taylor and Len Silverfine proudly view the Great Flag.

New York's Central Park, June 18, 1981.

Taken by one of Kodak's first panorama cameras and displayed across Grand Central Station's East Wall for weeks.

NBC's TODAY SHOW opened with the unfurling of the Flag's first stripe.

YOU'RE A GRAND OL' FLAG!

Stars & Stripes have a field day

ALL seven tons and two acres of America's largest flag were stretched out without a hitch yesterday in Central Park's Heckscher Field.

It took some two hours for the 400 volunteers to fully unfurl Old Glory — the flag's first public display since it welcomed the hostages home from Iran at Andrews Air Force Base in January.

The world's largest star spangled banner, which was made in Evanston, Ill., measures 411-by-211 feet and can fly 21 building stories high.

Yesterday's ceremony was the latest leg of a campaign to raise $650,000 required to install the special rigging needed to fly the polyester flag on the Verrazano-Narrows Bridge July 4.

That's where the flag was originally supposed to have flown on Bicentennial Day five years ago.

But it was torn apart by high winds before it had a chance to welcome the tall ships to New York Harbor for Op Sail.

But Operation Flag chairman Len Silverfine and the rest of the sponsors have never given up on their dream to give the flag a permanent home in the Big Apple.

Incidentally, here's how you can help: Send donations to Great American Flag Fund, P.O. Box F-L-A-G, New York, N.Y. 10022.

Among those on-hand for the unfurling were opera singer Robert Merrill and actress Elizabeth Taylor.

Len Silverfine, the man who wouldn't let the Operation Flag project die, stands before his glorious pride and joy.

Here it is in all its un

Victory! Young drive
cheers af

Central Park June 18, 1981, Dutch magazine spread provided by a friend living in Rotterdam.

Evening Magazine and the Today Show covered The Great Flag extensively.

Very little money was raised, however. We returned The Flag to storage at the Staten Island bridge anchorage, where it was to remain for 2 years. Central Park appeared to be the Great Flag's last hurrah.

—

Chapter XV:

The Whitehouse "Gifting"

When I started working on the Great American Flag, I was lecturing in marketing at McGill University's Faculty of Management and the University of Vermont's Business Department. I didn't have a lot of money, but I was solvent and happy, living a rather simple life with my German shepherd in a renovated barn that I owned with Bill in a Vermont ski resort town. We had since sold our property, and I had bought land further north, near the Canadian border, more convenient to my pre-flag weekly commute to Burlington and Montréal. And I was building a house out of wood salvaged from an old house and old barns farmers no longer used and were happy to give away for the taking. My dog had since died. I had given up teaching, though I loved doing it, as it conflicted with pursuing the Flag project. I was now out of work, and my savings were depleted.

To make myself whole again, I went back to work for a New York advertising agency, a life I had left 10 years earlier. But

'The Flag' would not go away. The new agency job was on a cosmetics account, coincidentally located in the General Motors building where Revlon's offices were. A couple months later, I was let go of that job because the client's president saw me talking with Paul Woolard, president of their rival Revlon, at the elevator bank in the G.M. building where both companies were headquartered. Paul, of course was the honorary chairman of The Great American Flag Fund, and we had just had lunch talking about how to infuse new energy into the project. Not a mention of the cosmetics business had transpired.

Everywhere I went, people asked me about 'The Flag.' Letters kept coming in that could not be answered. Many who knew me didn't ask at all so as not to embarrass me, but it was in their eyes. I might change my name and migrate to Australia (an old Ogilvy & Mather colleague who ran the Ogilvy agency in Melbourne said he could use me), but no, I didn't think 'it' was going to go away. There had to be a positive resolution.

Ironically, the Great Flag had, to a significant degree, achieved its basic objective. It had somehow risen from the stigma of the Bicentennial failure to become a seven-ton, 86,380 square-foot reality that made the front cover of the

"I am whatever you make me, nothing more. I am your belief in yourself, and your dream of what people may become. I am the day's work of the weakest man and the largest dream of the most daring. I am the clutch of an idea and the reasoned purpose of resolution. I am no more than you believe me to be, and I am all that you believe I can be. I am whatever you make me, nothing more."

If you look out at that grand Flag stretched behind us, you can see what we think of ourselves, our country, and our future. That Flag was made by and for men and women who still know how to dream great dreams and who still believe they can make their dreams come true. That giant banner was not created by a timid nation but by a bold one. Not a stitch was sewn in confusion or doubt. We understand that those stars and stripes stand for freedom and the forces of good. We apologize to no one for our ideals or our principles, nor for the prosperity that we've made for ourselves and shared with the world. Let this grand Flag forever be a symbol of the potential before us that free men and women can soar as high as their dreams, energy, and ambitions will take them.

On behalf of all Americans, I would like to thank the Great American Flag Fund and all the men and women who've made this inspiring gift possible. I promise you, that your government will keep it, treasure it, and use it as a reminder of the greatness that is America.

And now, if you will all join me, I would like to lead you in the Pledge of Allegiance.

[The President led the audience in the Pledge of Allegiance.]

I have to go now. I am leaving in that whirlybird for the Volunteer State, Tennessee. So, I'm looking forward to it for one reason, too. At the very start of the trip, I will get to see that magnificent Flag from above, from the air.

Thank you all very much. God bless you."

Note: The President spoke at 11:02 a.m. on the South Lawn. In his opening remarks, he referred to John H. Lyons, general president of the International Association of Bridge, Structural, and Ornamental Iron Workers of the AFL-CIO; J. Peter Grace, chairman and chief executive officer of W. R. Grace & Co.; and Len Silverfine, president of the Great American Flag Fund, Inc.

The 210-foot by 411-foot Flag was laid out on the Ellipse, behind the White House, for the ceremony as well as to mark Flag Day, 1983.

The Flag on the Ellipse, perfectly aligned on the north-south axis between The White House and The Jefferson Memorial.

The Great Flag's Scroll formalizing the gifting to the Government.

at the Monument well before Flag Day, June 14. Getting approval was no trouble as soon as I was able to obtain insurance, which I did. (This demand was a bit unusual, as how the heck do you insure a giant two-acre, seven-ton American Flag?) Nevertheless, I was able to find a friendly agent, and he secured the policy at no charge.

However, as it happened, the Gulf War ensued. Our victorious troops deserved a big homecoming. The GSA top brass suddenly realized they were the "owners" of The Great American Flag. Given the war the giant flag had extraordinary value to their director's and agency's image. At first, they reneged on their promise to release the Flag to be washed. Their spokeswoman, whom I had never dealt with because my contact had been a more junior manager, insisted there was no written agreement. In 15 years on the project, I had never felt the need to ask anyone to '*put it in writing,*' and nobody had ever asked it of me. I sensed trouble ahead.

Then, this spokesperson, probably realizing that she didn't need the task of washing 7 tons of fabric, relented, but only if we would agree to advance the washing schedule weeks to mid-March. With little choice, we advanced our schedule six weeks, hoping for the best from the weather. No luck. It was wet and cold for days after the washing.

Wilson Golf Ball Factory, Humboldt TN

For some reason (I suspect it was the thought our troops might be returning early), and without any prior notification, not a phone call to the Wilson plant, the GSA sent a semi-tractor to retrieve the Flag and its trailer, which was a bit strange as we had secured trucking (volunteered) to pick up the Flag in Washington, take it to Humboldt, and then to return the Flag to Washington when it was dry. Also, one would think that the GSA would have called the Wilson plant first to get a status report on the drying. They did not.

The Wilson plant manager, Al Scott, was taken completely by surprise and protested vigorously to the GSA truckers that the Flag was not dry. The truckers were quite insistent that they had their orders to pick up the Flag, so it was loaded into the Flag's trailer, still wet. Apparently, when the GSA transport returned to Washington, whatever the urgency had abated. *And no one at the GSA thought to open the trailer when it was returned!*

Finally opening the trailer weeks later and discovering a smelly, still damp Flag, the GSA looked around to lay blame elsewhere and used the occasion to dissociate The Flag from its history.

Recently, I told George, who remains a friend, that I was writing the story of The Great Flag and asked him if he would write some words about the Flag washing from Wilson's point of view.

His response:

The thing I love most about this phase of the Great American Flag's life is the purpose it's giving you.

The story you've authored about the Flag is, at its core, the story of America having a dream. Make it happen. Bring people along on that journey. There are a couple of paragraphs that can/should play a footnote in that story.

Bringing it out of hiding in 1990 after it was mothballed for eight years. Restoring it. Giving it another opportunity to cast its shadow and serve as a beacon for good. Those were some of the things that made the opportunity to get involved so attractive.

For a few weeks, Wilson Sporting Goods (an iconic American company and brand) contributed one of its factories and its workforce and became the world's largest laundromat.

There are mundane facts about how much water and detergent were used to clean the Flag, about how many people were engaged in the process, about how much airtime it got on local, regional, and national TV.

But what's not captured in that description is the pride and joy it brought to Humboldt, Tennessee. How hundreds of good people, led by Al Scott rallied around the mission of restoring the largest American Flag ever made to its rightful pristine condition.

It was a privilege and a joy to play a small part in enabling that to happen.

Thank you for giving me that opportunity.

— ***George Napier***

Seriously, does anyone believe that Wilson, Al Scott, the Wilson employees, and the citizens of Humboldt voluntarily shipped a wet Flag back to Washington without protest or warning?

———

Chapter XVII:

The "Re-Gifting" (a Seinfeld episode)

Needless to say, the GSA told a different story to the Washington newspapers and to the U.S. Marines who were enlisted to dry the Flag. Probing reporters got wind of the story and tracked me down in Vermont. I told them I would be pleased if the GSA honored the original agreement to store the Flag in between its annual display every Flag Day or on the Fourth and secured the permit for its display every year on the Monument grounds. However, I wagered that as soon as the GSA Director and his Public Relations staff had milked the Flag for its publicity value, it would be thrown back into storage, never to be seen again. I got it half-right. It went back into storage for a few years, and then GSA *re-gifted* The Flag to a space museum in Kansas.

Excuse me, but what were they thinking? This wasn't some ornament gifted at Christmas that didn't fit your home décor. You would think they might have wanted to ensure that the Great Flag was properly used as intended in its gifting. Had they done so, they would be the hero in this story. And perhaps, just perhaps, The Great Flag might have worked some of its magic to lessen our divisiveness and bring us together in common purpose.

—

I didn't hear any more about The Great Flag until the summer of 2001. Not surprisingly, the Kansas museum found no practical use for the huge Flag, so they offered it up for auction on eBay on July 4. A friend following the auction informed me that someone had purchased The Flag and its trailer for $12,300.

A little over two months later, as fate would have it, I received another call. *"Looks like your Flag has been displayed in western Pennsylvania."* The caller read the news blurb, which mentioned "a 7-ton flag." It had to be the Great Flag. I called the Kansas Museum. The director gave me the buyer's name and telephone number. I left a voicemail message. My call was returned within minutes.

"*Ted Dorfman. I've been trying to locate you for weeks. My wife and I saw the Flag on eBay. We knew its story. 'Couldn't stand the thought that it might get into the wrong hands, so we bought it along with the trailer. It's been sitting here near our house. United #93 went down in a field just miles from where we live. We thought it appropriate to honor the victims by displaying the Great Flag in a nearby field. The whole town, the fire department, everybody pitched in. The Flag is in great shape. Don't you worry; we intend to take good care of it."*

And so, they have: The Dorfmans established a website for The Great Flag, https://www.greatamericanflag.org, and have faithfully continued The Flag's legacy and care. Josh, their son, and his childhood friend AJ Rehberg have since assumed responsibility.

Call me a romantic, but I think Carl Sandburg got it just right.

—

Email from Josh Dorfman in December 2022:

Hi Len,

Great to hear from you! Of course, we wish it would have been under different circumstances. What a tragedy about your apartment fire! I am terribly sorry to hear of the trouble that must have been caused and also saddened by the loss of your Flag records. I am envisioning a mini museum in your home, and it's terrible to think of that being gone. I imagine the entire ordeal must be devastating for you.

Regarding the Washington Post article, we never interpreted it as critical of you. In fact, we viewed it as a testament to your decades-long dedication to the Flag and frustrating encounters with the GSA. We see you as an inspiration and have worked to portray you that way in every medium in which we discuss you and the Flag. We believe your story needs to be told accurately and with respect.

We are continually impressed by your meticulous chronicling of the Flag's history and trust that you have accurate records from the decades. As such, we have honored your request to remove the article from our site and hope to replace it with another that tells the story more accurately. If you have any suggestions, we are open to them!

I will admit a little embarrassment on my part that we have not given our mission the proper attention since the pandemic started. We love the mission and believe in what we are doing, but admittedly, this has been on the back burner, and that has been a source of stress for me. Please know we are committed and hope to continue the legacy you created.

Your friend,

Josh

Epilogue:

Thank you for reading UNLESS FIRST WE DREAM. I hope you not only enjoyed the story but that it inspires your vision of this place we call America. We, Americans, are not the natural consequence of history left to its own devices, (monarchies were the norm when we began), but an ideal that requires conscious and continuing nurture on the part of all its citizens, in general agreement, to be realized and maintained.

Without continuing our collective dream, that of the 'shining city on the hill,' reinforcing and enriching itself further, we cannot hope to be the United States. And without being united one must ask: Can we survive in a Darwinian world where only the fittest do? I fear we will decline and pass into history, as other prominent nations in past centuries have, unable to hold course to their founding inspiration.

I would like to close with regard to the meaning of a few pertinent words: "in unison", "united", "together", etc., in the context of our democratic republic...

Common sense and our Founders tell us there cannot be a divided United States. Why? Aside from being an oxymoron, history informs us that large nations prey on small/divided/weaker nations.

So, where does that leave us? Guess what?

We're married! All fifty of us! (In fact, it is even more complicated, all 330 million of us.) And, if we were to go into marriage counseling, what would the counselor advise…

"You must do better at compromise and working together to find solutions."

"You may think you are right, and you may in fact be right, or righter than the other, but if you do not in sincerity, and with respect, seek to work toward and reach compromise with the other side of the issue…

"You are wrong! Terribly wrong, and destructive of the entity you both pretend to care about and can dissolve only with great peril."

I have nothing against the business of marriage counseling, but let's save our money to be put to better use and get our act together! Divorce is not an option. Nor is continued disunity. The Putins, Ayatollahs, and Xi Jinping's of the world are always hungry, and they eagerly await. The only path in our Darwinian world is to be the fittest, or at least fit enough not to be challenged. *If we wish to survive then, we need to reward politicians that bring us together, not those that further our divisiveness.*

Ah, you do not like that? You should have read the ~~memo~~ Preamble…

*We, the People of the United States, in Order to form **a more perfect Union**, establish Justice, ensure domestic tranquility, provide for the common defense...*

They knew it couldn't be perfect.

—

One more thought, I am not familiar with the current syllabi being taught in our schools today, but I do hear from friends, and I do talk to their children. And I see a lack of knowledge of, as well as interest in history—not just the when, but the why, what was the effect, and how better outcomes could have been attained. Ignorance of history is a sure way of repeating its mistakes.

And please, the next time you see our Flag, no matter its size, stop and think about what it really represents and of all those who have fought and died for our collective dream to succeed.

Sincerely,

Len Silverfine

P.S. I hope you will join me and others in getting our government to fulfill the promise it made in 1983, and allow Americans, particularly grandparents, parents, and their children to unfurl this Great Flag every year as it is pictured on the front cover.